COLUMBUS' SHIPS

COLUMBUS' SHIPS

by

JOSÈ MARIA MARTINEZ-HIDALGO

Edited

by

HOWARD I. CHAPELLE

BARRE PUBLISHERS

BARRE, MASSACHUSETTS, 1966

List of Illustrations

Contents

Foreword

The ships that brought Columbus to the "New World," and opened the American continent to exploration, settlement and development are naturally of interest to those Americans concerned with the history of the evolution of shipping in the United States. It is very difficult, however, for an American to make a study of these vessels for the information that would be of value does not exist in this country. Hence the student must search abroad.

Due to the state of the art and science of naval architecture and shipbuilding in the time of Columbus, neither plans nor scale models of ships of this period exist. In addition, though we are able to identify the types of vessels used by Columbus, we are not sure of their exact size.

With such handicaps it requires long studies of material, ranging from ill-proportioned representations of vessels in works of art, sketches, paintings and sculptures to very rare votive models. Incomplete, non-technical descriptions of ships of the 15th century can be found, but these are too often exaggerated and imaginative rather than factual.

It is the good fortune of today that a Spaniard, who is a naval officer, a yachtsman and a scholar, undertook this study about a decade ago. As the Director of the Museo Maritimo at Barcelona, he began work with the objective of having scale exhibition models built of Columbus' ships.

Thus prepared, Capitan de Corbetta Jose M. Martinez-Hidalgo began the long, often tedious, search for evidence regarding 15th century Spanish ships of the types that made up the squadron for Columbus' first voyage of discovery. By careful analysis of available evidence, with due regard to the requirements of a ship of Columbus' squadron, numerous conclusions could be reached.

This work traces the development of these conclusions, as well as presenting a great deal of the basic evidence and source. As a result, the ships can be reconstructed with at least reasonable accuracy, as to appearance, general model and rig of each.

Along the course of Martinez-Hidalgo's work, the opportunity arose to design and supervise the construction of the *Santa Maria* in full size, as an exhibit in the New York World's Fair of 1964-65, for an American owner, Mr. Lawrence Vineburgh. This gave additional information and corrections which would not be possible had only a model been built.

Through Mr. Vineburgh's desire to have a professional American consultant, the Smithsonian Institution allowed me to visit the *Santa Maria* reconstruction at numerous times during construction. This also permitted me to follow much of Martinez-Hidalgo's research and to consider the basis of the more important of his conclusions and opinions.

As a result, the publication of the lines and sail plans of the vessels became desirable and, with the aid of Mr. Vineburgh, Capitan de Corbetta Martinez-Hidalgo's manuscript was translated into English and prepared for publication.

Having had the opportunity to follow the research, the model construction and, finally, the *Santa Maria* reconstruction, I am convinced that the new presentations of the reconstruction of each of Columbus' vessels are advances on previous efforts, in all respects.

Howard I. Chapelle
Curator of Transportation
Smithsonian Institution
United States National Museum
Washington, D.C.

PART I

Background and Reconstruction

I. *THE PATH TO LA RABIDA*

I N THE middle of the year of grace 1485, a ship arriving from Lisbon dropped anchor in the Tinto River, opposite the village of Palos de la Frontera, or Palos de Moguer, as that once active river port of the Province of Huelva is now alternately called. Huelva was one of the most important maritime centers of Andalucia, having a large fleet of caravels and in sharp competition with the Portuguese in both ship construction and in trade with the west coast of Africa.

From this ship, a man about 30 years old, tall, strongly built, of ruddy complexion, blue eyes, aquiline nose, prominent cheek bones, and red hair beginning to turn white, disembarked. By his clothes, he looked like a pilgrim about to begin begging, but in his piercing stare there was fire, in his speech, decision, and in his manner, self-assurance.

Taking the steep and isolated path that led to the ancient Moorish fortress of La Rabida; then as now a Franciscan monastery; the man led a small boy, of about five years of age, to the monastery door. Arriving at the brick entrance warmed by the sun and with whitewashed walls, the stranger knocked and on the door being opened, whispered a prayer to the Virgin, and then entered with the boy. These two were to become the first and second "Admirals of the Indies."

The man was Christopher Columbus; sailor, trader and navigator of distant seas. He had left his birthplace and relations many years before and, in his roamings had been shipwrecked in Portugal. Here he had obtained some knowledge of cosmography and had also acquired the grammar and language of the first great Portuguese writer Camoens, as well as that of the first noted Spanish author, Berceo. He had also learned some Latin, the latter being then very desirable due to its prestige in social and intellectual circles.

The boy, Columbus' son Diego, was to become the second "Admiral of the Indies". He had probably been born in Porto Santo, Portugal, sometime about 1480. The mayor of Porto Santo had been the brother of Diego's mother, Filipa Perestello Moniz, whom Columbus married in Portugal. The boy was to receive education in the royal court and to become related to the Royal House of Castile by his marriage to Maria de Toledo, niece of the Duke of Alba. When Diego became viceroy his wife received the unusual honor of being allowed to have gold and jewels on the saddle and trappings of the horses on which she might ride.

The stranger, welcomed in Spain by Franciscan charity, was the incarnation of tremendous will-power, with perseverance bordering on stubborness combined with great sagacity. Columbus was convinced that there was a great destiny for Castile; he believed that the kingdom was to accomplish a mission of world importance. But he knew that Isabel I, dominant in the Royal Family, would be influenced only by religion, rather than by promises of spices or of the wealth of King Solomon's mines. Therefore, Columbus approached with a promise that his project would lead to the expansion of Christianity. This proved to be the factor that inclined the Queen to place her faith in the adventurous navigator.

As a result of this faith, and Columbus' great project, Castile and all of Spain eventually gave language, culture and religion, yes and blood too, to over twenty nations. The glory of Spain is in the great geographical discovery that she alone made, transcending all that had previously been accomplished and comparable to the exploration of space in modern times.

II. *THE MOST FAMOUS SHIP IN THE WORLD*

This unparalleled venture, leading to the discovery of the New World, was carried out in Spanish designed and built ships, financed entirely by Spanish funds, manned and equipped by Spaniards and commanded by a captain selected and commissioned by the Royal House of Spain. This officer, though not born in Spain, had become a citizen of Spain by his own free choice.

The flagship of the audacious little squadron, the *Santa Maria*, has become famous — more so than any ship since *Noah's Ark* (but the latter was apparently more raft than ship, having no means of propulsion). The *Santa Maria*, and the commander and crew on board her, influenced the world more than any ship and crew, and perhaps, more than any single space vehicle may ever do.

When the science of marine archaeology was first established, perhaps by Auguste Jal in 1840, one of the primary problems was the reconstruction of the *Santa Maria;* then her companions, the *Pinta* and *Nina* had to be considered.

In the period when the *Santa Maria* was built, and for some time afterward, the art of naval architecture followed accepted rules that had been established by centuries of trial and error, apparently without accurate and detailed drawings. The traditions of the shipbuilders, formed to the music of the ship carpenters' tools, were the real guides, rather than theories. The controlling factor in design and construction was the use requirements. These were established by careful observations made during countless voyages.

Also, the captains and pilots all contributed their comments and opinions on the relative behavior of ships in a given trade. This happened in Spain and elsewhere.

It should be noted that the earliest English plans known, probably based on Venetian practice of ship design, date from 1586: known as the *Fragments of English Shipwrightery* now preserved in the Pepysian Library, Magdalene College, Cambridge, England, they are commonly credited to Matthew Baker, the famous Elizabethan master shipwright.

Precise plans of ships were slow in development, for it was not until the 17th century that reasonably complete construction plans were made and not until the last decade of the 18th century that fully complete and accurate working plans for building a ship were developed and in general use.

The design and construction details of Columbus' ships must now be based upon the very limited information contained in the journal of his first trip to the New World, combined with contemporary, or nearly contemporary, sketches, paintings, masonry carvings, medals, seals, engravings and other individually inadequate sources. One very important source is a church, or votive, model nearly contemporary with the *Santa Maria*. Other information can be acquired from naval and maritime archives, travellers' accounts and historians' statements, but all are lacking in technical precision. Contemporary art representations are usually the work of artists lacking in maritime knowledge and are drawn without proper regard to scale or proportions. Early books on ship construction and naval architecture may ocasionally be useful, but they are all of much later date than the Columbian period and many are very limited in scope. These works are generally more theoretical than practical.

In other words, the scholar must interpret the available information with care, for some of the references are overly influenced by national pride or by ignorance of practical wooden shipbuilding. Only by careful analysis and objective study, a search for new reference material and trial and error reconstructions employing selected data, can a marine archeological examination of the ships of Columbus' squadron be made with a satisfactory degree of accuracy in all important respects. This method alone will insure sound opinions regarding the characteristics of the nao and the caravels.

III. *COLUMBUS' JOURNAL OR LOGBOOK*

After 1524, all Spanish navigators were required to maintain a logbook or journal of their voyages. This was intended to produce a record of their movements and to enable authorities to keep abreast of nautical exploration and trade developments. But seamen were reluctant to write complete accounts of their voyages; some because they were not well educated and therefore wrote poorly and laboriously. Others did not take the time to report thoroughly. For those reasons the journals or logbooks were not satisfactory, and later Phillip II found it necessary to reinforce the orders concerning journals, in his ordinances relative to maritime discoveries.

Columbus, however, anticipated the voyage journal requirement and, on returning from his first voyage, he presented to the King in Barcelona a manuscript journal or log, with the daily occurrences fully recorded.

The original log was considered a state secret and steps were taken in order that its contents would not become known to foreigners, Portugal in particular. Portugal, above all other countries, was most interested in exploration and discovery and was constantly searching for information on the explorations of Castile. The reverse was also true. The Columbus manuscript log became the exclusive property of the Catholic King, who returned to Columbus a copy of the original prepared by two trusted secretaries and prepared with great secrecy.

The steps taken to protect this journal were so effective that, even now, the whereabouts of the original document is wholly unknown.

Hence a letter, in which Columbus had made a resume of his first voyage, dated on board the *Nina* February 15, 1493, was the first information made public. This was widely distributed almost immediately by means of a pamphlet published at Barcelona in April of this year. A month later a Latin translation appeared in Rome, followed by other publications in Valladolid, Basel, Antwerp, Paris and Strasbourg in Spanish, Latin and French during the next four years. Even a poetical version appeared in Florence and there are references to the existence of translations in the Catalonian language (which have now disappeared) among the books in the library of Ferdinand Columbus.

The Columbus letter had been sent to five different destinations — the Catholic King, Gabriel Sanchez, Luis de Santangel, the Duke of Medinaceli and the Cordova city government. They were sent, it appears, from Lisbon and the last one from Palos on the 15th of March 1493. This last one was publicly read a week later and produced so much interest that the bearer was paid

The islands discovered by Columbus. Engraving in the edition of the Columbus letter to Gabriel Sanchez, Basel, 1493.

1,000 maravedises and presented with a new doublet. Cordova, where Beatriz Enriquez de Arana, mother of Ferdinand Columbus had lived, was proud of being able to call the great navigator "neighbor" and also for having contributed two men to the crew of the *Santa Maria*. One was Diego de Arana, a cousin of Beatriz, who served on the *Santa Maria* as a captain's clerk. The other was a surgeon, Juan Sanchez. Both were left in the Fortress de la Navidad in the West Indies, from which they never returned.

The copy of the logbook retained by Columbus was supposed, with some reason, to have been in the possession of his grandson, Luis, as he had plans for publishing it in 1554 (?). However, this was not done, for some reason, and the log may have been included in the 15,000 volumes in the magnificent library that his father, Ferdinand, a man of great erudition and a careful collector, had left to him. It was apparently from this library, first left to the librarian of the Dominicans of St. Paul and later to the librarian of the Cathedral of Seville, that the able Las Casas made his famous extracts of the *Book of the First Navigation and Discovery of the Indies,* [on finding the copy made at Barcelona when he was in the Monastery of St. Paul (1552) and before he was consecrated Bishop of Chiappas] for his *History of the Indies.* The original manuscript of this book is in the National Library, Madrid, Section of Manuscripts, reference R. 21.

The original extracts of Las Casas, generally called *The Columbus Journal,* were found by Martin Fernandez de Navarette in 1791 in the library of the Duke of Infantado and are now preserved in the Spanish National Library, Section of Manuscripts, reference Vol. 6, Number 7. Fernandez de Navarette published these in 1825, in the first volume of his *Collection of the Voyages and Discoveries by Sea Made by the Spaniards Since the End of the 15th Century,* after correcting some errors relating to navigation, but making some paleographical mistakes of his own.

Fr. Bartolome de las Casas apparently made a literal copy of the parts of the manuscript log that he considered most important. Unfortunately, his point of view was not that of a sailor and much less that of a modern archeologist. In his extract he apparently abbreviated some passages, and attempted to correct what he thought were mistakes. He also amplified the original extracts with marginal notes in great number, bringing sharp comments from such later critics as Vignaud, Janes, Carbia and others.

Today it is generally accepted that the Friar tried to make an honest transcription as far as he thought sufficient. In general, he used the third person, singular or plural, but in some sentences he used the first person and it seems that where this occurred, particularly in some extensive paragraphs, the real Columbus speaks. However, references like that to Florida, on November 21st in the log extract, are examples of Las Casas' mistakes, for Florida was not discovered until 1513. Some of his mistakes may be due to the errors in copying in the basic document available to him, or to imperfect handwriting of the royal secretaries, about which Las Casas complained, but he was prone to mistakes himself. This makes it necessary to use the Las Casas extract with some caution.

Nevertheless, the log extract appears to be a generally correct copy of the working logbook, omitting attempts at correction and addition. This is shown by the use of normal expressions growing out of Columbus' stay in Portugal, Madeira, Porto Santo, etc., such as words of the lingua Franca (the primitive slang or jargon of Mediterranean sailors), as well as other words from the Atlantic coast, Portuguese and even some "Americanisms" from the New World, which he introduced into Castilian, such as "canoe", "cacique", "hammock" and "shark".

For the reconstruction of the *Santa Maria* and other Columbus vessels, the extract of Las Casas is still a primary source, authoritative and suggestive at the very least.

Thanks to the journal of Columbus there can be no doubt as to the rigs and sails of the ships; the information in the journal amounting, perhaps, to as much as 50% of the available specific knowledge of the vessels. From the known contemporary rules for proportioning the dimensions of vessels, it can be deduced that the rig had influence on the lines of the hull and that the rig of the nao must relate to its hull-form, whose proportions were 1-2-3. Thus, reasonable assumptions can be made as to the hull-form of the *Santa Maria*.

This is likewise the case with the *Pinta* and *Nina* whose rigs and rigging changes are mentioned in the journal; a fairly accurate conception of their design can be obtained. A caravel-rigged vessel would normally have hull-proportions of 1-2-3.33, rather than the 1-2-3 of the nao.

Specific information exists as to the awkwardness and draft of the *Santa Maria*, compared with the easy handling, light draft and good sailing qualities of the *Pinta* and *Nina;* to the forecastle of the flagship; to the types of each of the vessels; to *Santa Maria* as a nao with a topsail, *Pinta* as a round caravel, and the *Nina* as a lateen caravel (later changed at Las Palmas to a round caravel) ; to the small boats, barca and batel; to the armament, bombards, cross-bows and pikes; to the navigating compasses and to observations in magnetic declination. It has been suggested that Columbus discovered the phenomenon of the declination, but this had been mentioned by Chaucer in his *Treatise on the Astrolabe,* 1380, and perhaps indicated in the Atlas of Andria Bianco, 1451, and also in a sun dial of 1451, in the Museum of Innsbruck. Declination is certainly mentioned in an engraved pamphlet at Nurnburg in the same year as Columbus' discovery of the New World.

The Las Casas extract also mentions such things as the sand glass, navigating quadrant and astrolabe, the sounding lead, some of the ship dressings of the nao and caravels, such as flags and heraldic arms, royal standards and flags having a green cross, the distinctive signal of the famous flotilla.

IV. *RECONSTRUCTIONS OF THE SANTA MARIA*

There are hundreds of models of the *Santa Maria,* Columbus' flagship, spread about the museums of the world and in private collections. Many of them are based upon the Spanish reconstructions of 1892. Too many, however, are the product of enthusiastic model builders who were without research facilities and material and who relied largely on imagination.

The reconstructions based on original research which deserve the attention of the marine archeologist can be limited to four:

1. Those of the Spanish Commission of 1892. The Commission was presided over by the well-known historian and naval captain Cesareo Fernandez Duro. The occasion was the preparation for the fourth centennial of the discovery of America.

2. Those of Enrico D'Albertis, 1892. These studies and plans were presented in Vol. 4 of the *la Raccolta di Documenti e Studi* published by the Royal Commissione Columbiana, Rome, under the auspices of the Italian government. After seeing the results of the Spanish commission's work he modified some of his ideas and, by order of the city government of Genoa, he made small scale models of the ships for the maritime museum at Pegli.

3. The reconstruction of the *Santa Maria* by Naval Lt. Julio F. Guillen, 1927, for the Ibero-American Exposition in Seville, 1929.

4. The reconstruction in a scale model by R. C. Anderson, 1930, for the Addison Gallery of American Art, Phillips Academy, Andover, Massachusetts, U.S.A.

The only full-size reconstructions built to the best judgment of the proponent of each, are the Spanish efforts of Fernandez Duro and Julio Guillen, each of whom faced difficult problems of construction, interior arrangement and workable rigging that are not usually met in a scale model.

All of those who have been mentioned, except Guillen, considered the *Santa Maria* to have been a nao. Guillen, to the surprise of most marine archeologists, considered the ship to be a caravel.

It should be mentioned that Raphael Monleon y Torres, restorer of paintings in the Naval Museum at Madrid and a member of the 1892 Spanish Commission, made plans for a *Santa Maria* and also made plans for the two caravels of the 1892 reconstruction of Columbus' flotilla.

V. *SANTA MARIA OF THE SPANISH COMMISSION OF 1892*

This reconstruction is popularly called that of Fernandez Duro because he was the Chairman of the Spanish Commission of 1892. The calculations for stability and for the rig were done by the Chief of the Naval Engineers, Casimiro Bona, who was also in charge of the preliminary study group. Fernandez Duro and the artist Raphael Monleon were members of this group. The other members of the Commission were Commander Emilio Ruiz de Arbol, as secretary, and Aureliano Fernandez-Guerra and Juan de Dios de la Rada y Delgado, who represented the Royal Academy of History.

The reconstruction was supervised by the naval architect Leopoldo Puente, draftsman of the plans of this first attempt at reconstruction. The vessel was launched at the arsenal of La Carraca (Cadiz) the 26th of June 1892, 63 days after laying the keel. The work was carried on rapidly in order for the vessel to take the principal part in the commemoration ceremonies of the fourth centenary of the discovery of America, in the presence

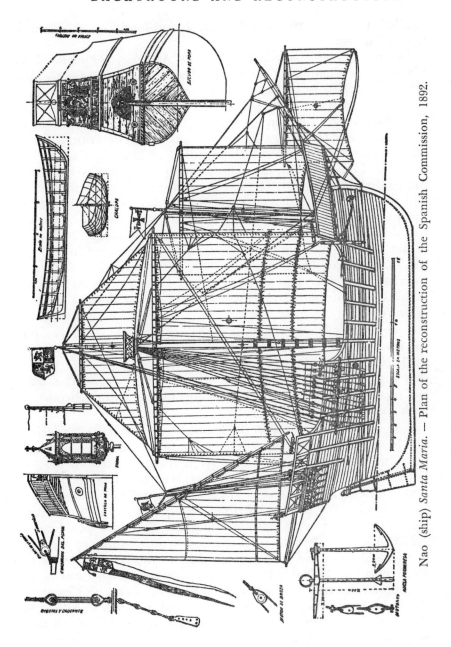

Nao (ship) *Santa Maria.* — Plan of the reconstruction of the Spanish Commission, 1892.

I 2

of a brilliant representation of Spanish and foreign naval authorities, at Huelva.

Later, the nao was sailed across the Atlantic, commanded by Commander Victor M. Concas; the destination being the Columbian World Fair at Chicago; the vessel being the gift of Spain.

The nao sailed from Santa Cruz de Tenerife, on the 22nd of February, 1893. The voyage was far more difficult than that of Columbus, due to the weather conditions, which deteriorated soon after departure. When the 21st parallel of latitude was reached in the middle of March, the nao met with very heavy weather and the rolling and pitching of the ship became so violent that resort had to be made to oil poured on the sea, to reduce the force of the waves. With strong winds and heavy seas on her beam, the nao showed a tendency to run off to leeward, at nearly 90 degrees to her course. In spite of this, she made the crossing in one day less than Columbus. On March 30th the nao reached San Juan, Puerto Rico. Her best day's run had been 139 miles and her poorest 11. She sailed to Havana and was towed from there to New York.

Fernandez Duro decided that the *Santa Maria* was a nao, basing his argument on the extracts of Columbus' journal. This was his basic and sound conclusion, founded on specific references to that document. Over the years, the theory of Fernandez Duro has received the support of historians and marine archeologists, with but few exceptions.

By deduction, based on the length of the longboat, he arrived at a basis of the main dimensions of the hull; like Jal, he thought that the length of the boat was given in the extract of the logbook. This was a mistake however, as will be explained at some length later. Monleon also made this mistake in his study of the caravels. For the rest, Fernandez Duro took his inspiration from Diego Garcia de Palacio and Juan Escalante de Mendoza (see Bibliography) producing, as a result, a ship more appropriate to the middle of the 16th century than to the last quarter of the 15th century. This can be seen not only in the hull but in the rig, too advanced for a ship of the Columbian era. For example, the bulwarks of the forecastle were curved, in plan, to follow the shape of the forebody, producing an appearance for which there was no precedence, for the bulwarks had been straight in plan view earlier than about the middle of the 16th century. Perhaps the most noticeable mistake of the Fernandez Duro *nao* was too much use of ornamental details, whereas, in the Columbian era, the style was austere; especially in a merchant ship. The use of a square stern was not seen in naos, even though used in caravels in the Columbian era. It is not until the Turkish map of Piri-Reis, 1513, was made, that such a stern is indicated. Fernandez Duro designed the stern in accordance to that shown in a map of the Spanish cartographer, Diego Rivero, 1529. Further, on this authority, he made the main topsail of trapezoidal form, sheeting to the main yard arms. On the whole, his reconstruction resembles more a Dutch ship of the period 1540-50 than a Spanish ship of the Columbian period. The general characteristics of the reconstruction of 1892 are the following: Length on the keel, 18.5 meters; length on the load water line, 21.76 meters; length between perpendiculars, 22.6 meters; length overall, 39.10 meters (this data is taken from the report of the Commission and the overall length is from bowsprit end to mizzen sheet boomkin); extreme breadth, 7.84 meters; depth from the bottom of the keel to the height of the main deck at the side, 3.80 meters; draft, fore 2.18 meters, aft 3.02 meters. The displacement of the vessel, on these dimensions, was 233 tons. The length of the mainmast is given as 27.25 meters.

VI *SANTA MARIA OF D'ALBERTIS*, 1892-94

Captain D'Albertis, in his "Le construzioni navale e L'arte de la Navigazione al Tempo de C. Colombo", included in Vol. 4, *Raccolta di Documenti e Studi pubblicati dalla R. Commissione Colombiana* (Rome, 1892-94), presented to the public his studies of Columbus' ships, accompanied by plans. In attempting to deduce the principal dimensions of the *Santa Maria,* Captain D'Albertis did not make the mistake, as have others, of accepting Jal's assumption regarding the length of the ship's boat, as a basic reference for the size of the nao. Rather, he established his position on the base of crew size. He assumed a crew of forty, which can be accepted as correct. But he was much influenced by the work of the Spanish author Escalante de Mendoza (see Bibliography) of 1571, of much later date than the Columbian era, and also by Garcia del Palacio, 1587, (see Bibliography). His estimate of tonnage is 179 tons in spite of the fact that the notable Asturian Captain, del Palacio, was clearly stating that the *Santa Maria* of Columbus was about 100 tons.

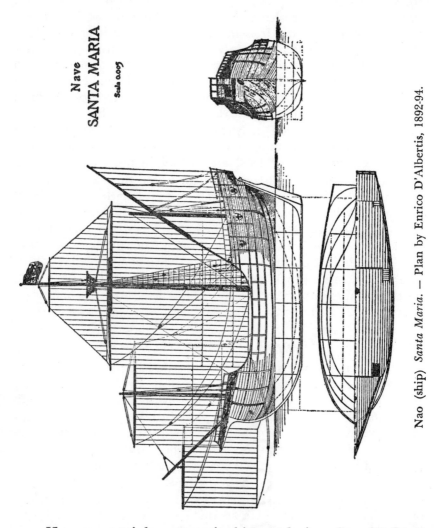

Nao (ship) *Santa Maria*. – Plan by Enrico D'Albertis, 1892-94.

He was certainly correct in his conclusion that the *Santa Maria* was a nao and in giving her a round-tuck stern and a forecastle whose bulwarks were straight in plan at the sides. But his concept of three vertical masts, and his spar proportions are far more appropriate for ships of nearly a half century later than to

Columbus' ships. By 1540 the mainmast no longer was the really important mast, carrying the most effective propelling sail, with fore and mizzen mere balancing and steering sails. By this date the fore and mizzen sails had become larger in proportion to the mainsail and contributed more to the propelling force, than in the time of Columbus.

The rigging is incomplete in the plans accompanying the D'Albertis report, and the stern cabin was not shown, though added later in the scale model made from the plans. The upper stay leads to the topmast head, the lift of the lateen yard mizzen leads to the same place, the backstays of the mainmast, the double sheets, foresail braces lead to the mainstay; these are not practical in the handling of vessels of the Columbian era. The principal dimensions of the *Santa Maria* of D'Albertis are:

Length on deck	26.3	meters
Length of keel	19.0	meters
Extreme breadth	8.4	meters
Depth in hold	4.5	meters
Draft at stern	2.9	meters
Height of mainmast, heel to cap	28.7	meters
Length of mainyard	19.0	meters
Capacity	179	toneles (tonel was equivalent of 5/6 of a measurement ton).

VII. *SANTA MARIA OF GUILLEN TATO,* 1927-29

This is the sole reconstruction of the *Santa Maria* as a caravel. The proposal to build this ship developed when the Ibero-American Fair of Seville (1929) was being planned. The ship was the project of the then Lieutenant Julio F. Guillen Tato, author of *La Carabela Santa Maria* (1927). This publication shows that the author's use of documentary evidence produced quite a different assumption that did not agree with Fernandez Duro and D'Albertis, as to the type of ship employed as Columbus' flagship.

The caravel was built in the Echevarietta Shipyard at Cadiz under the direction of the projector in accordance with the plans prepared for him by Chief of Engineers of the Spanish Navy, Jose Quintana. These plans have never been published and the Ger-

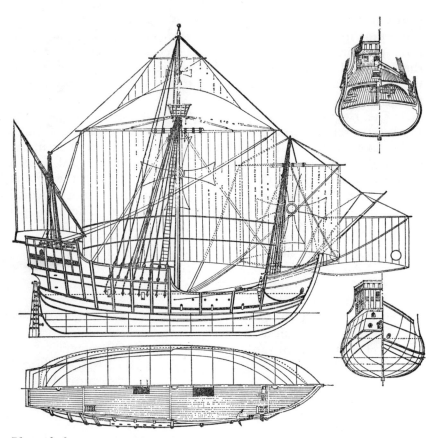

Plan of the reconstruction of the *Santa Maria,* as a caravel, by Julio F. Guillén, 1929.

man scholar, Heinrich Winter, expressed his displeasure on this matter. (see Bibliography).

After serving as an exhibit at the Fair at Seville, the caravel was anchored at Sebo Point, opposite the Monastery of la Rabida. In 1945 the vessel was towed from Valencia to Cartagena in order to make some repairs, but on the way the vessel sank, due to her weak state.

A copy of this ship was built at Valencia by the Lacomba Shipyard in 1951 for the principal purpose of employing her in making the cinema *Alba de America.* Taken to Barcelona in 1952, the vessel has been moored opposite the Columbus Monument in Atarazanas dock so that it can be visited by the public. In 1957 the Navy Ministery presented the vessel to the Provincial Deputies of Barcelona, with its supervision made the responsibility of the Director of the Maritime Museum there.

Contrary to the opinion of the great majority of historians, marine archeologists and other scholars, the author chose to consider the vessel to be a caravel, basing his reasoning on such claims as "tradition", statements in some scholarly books and upon two quotations from the extract of Columbus' journal. In a later chapter we will discuss this matter at some length. Guillen also deduced the length of the ship by what he assumed to be the length of her boat — "five fathoms" — and he believed the boat to have been stowed lengthwise, and taking up the whole length of the waist of the ship, though such stowage could well have required more or less space.

The "length of the boat" theory first appeared in Jal's book, and was followed by Fernandez Duro, as we have mentioned, and then by Guillen. For the moment it will be sufficient to say that this theory is the result of a misinterpretation of the passage in the journal, under the date of Tuesday, November 27, where Columbus is made to say "He found an entrance of a river that was wide enough for a galley to pass through and entering it the total length of that boat it had five and eight fathoms." The correct interpretation seems to be that Columbus penetrated the river mouth a distance equal to the length of the boat and then found depths of water of 5 to 8 fathoms. This version is supported by Ferdinand Columbus later, when he says that Columbus had entered "quato importaba la lunghez a della barca appunto; ove trovai fondo di cinque fine ad octo braccia."

If the interpretation accepted by Jal, Fernandez Duro and Guillen was correct, some days after November 27th (on December 6th) in the journal, there would be the statement: "So much as the length of an oar of a boat, it was five fathoms." So that we have a boat oar of nearly 30 feet! It should be noted that R. C. Anderson, in discussion of his model, stated that "fathoms" were employed only in measuring depths of water or lengths of cable and rope, but were not used for linear measurement of ships and boats generally. Rather, shipbuilding measurements were in cubits or feet in Spain until the metric system was introduced.

Professor Samuel Morison, referring to this mistake of three authorities in fixing the dimensions of the *Santa Maria,* said that, basing his statement on the principal of the restoration of the mammoth starting with the jaw, Auguste Jal proposed, in 1840, to reconstruct the dimensions of the *Santa Maria,* taking as the initial point the length of the rowing boat—the five fathoms which supposedly Columbus mentioned in his journal — but, unfortunately in doing this he took a false jaw. The five fathoms mentioned referred to the depth of water in the mouth or entrance of the river and harbor of Baracoa, measured from a rowboat, and does not refer to the length of the boat, in Anderson's opinion.

From the assumed length of the ship's boat, Guillen calculated the length of the waist of the ship, supporting this by reference to Garcia del Palacio of nearly a century later than 1492, by which time the ships had changed a great deal. Palacio claimed that the naos had a small boat, 'y ha de tener el batel del largo que tuviese la fuga de la tolda hasta la afrizada del castillo de proa . . . ", or a boat of length that would stow between the break of the quarter deck and the break of the forecastle. This idea is not only incorrect because of the error regarding the length of the boat, but also because the waist was shorter toward the end of the 15th century (as can be seen in the Mataro nao, in La Carrack by "W A", in the nao of *Libre del Consolat* and in the sketches on the map of Juan de la Cosa, to give but a few references), than in the naos described by Palacio.

For the rest, Guillen depended upon *Livro Nautico,* the famous anonymous Portuguese manuscript, which contains information on caravels of the 16th century, the dates varying from 1575 to 1591. In adddition, he also used to some extent the publications of Lopes de Mendoca, member of the Portuguese Commission for the commemoration of the fourth centenary of the discovery of the New World.

The rig can be considered accurate, with the exception of the main topsail, taken from Diego Rivero. The poop cabin is based on the well known *Oceanica Classis* and was more suited to the period of Columbus than in the 1892 reconstruction. The principal dimensions were:

Length on deck .... 25.7 meters
Length of keel .... 18.7 meters

Extreme Breadth .... 7.5 meters
Depth in hold .... 3.3 meters
Draft at the stern .... 2.2 meters
Length of the mainmast, from
    keel to cap .... 28.0 meters
Length of mainyard .... 18.0 meters
Capacity .... 120 toneles (1 tonel
                                                    equals 5/6 of a ton
                                                    (measurement)

VIII. *SANTA MARIA OF R. C. ANDERSON,* 1930

This reconstruction was made in a small scale model, such as was used by D'Albertis, hence there was not the great number of problems in construction and rigging found in a full-size reconstruction. Anderson, the distinguished English marine research authority, gave some data on his model in *The Mariner's Mirror* (Vol. XVI, No. 2, April 1930), based on his research and opinions. His *Santa Maria* was a nao, with proper proportions for the period and correctly rigged. The main topsail was not trapezoidal as in the previous versions, but square, small, without a gored foot as shown in Carpaccio.

The proportions of the "pena" (upper part) and "car" (lower and thicker part) of the mizzen lateen yard, and the sheet of the topsail running through the blocks on the arms of the main yard, I consider incorrect. The capacity of the hull and the draft seem excessive. The principal dimensions are:

Length on deck .... 24.7 meters
Length of keel .... 16.5 meters
Extreme breadth .... 8.2 meters
Depth in hold .... 4.1 meters
Draft of vessel .... 3.3 meters
Length of mainmast, keel to cap .... 24.7 meters
Length of mainyard .... 19.5 meters

The displacement, the centers of buoyancy and of gravity, scantlings, draft, and other data are not given. Therefore it cannot be determined whether or not the ship represented by this model would sail and work as would the original vessel. The model builder, like the artist, is free of these problems at least.

IX. *THE CARAVELS*

In the great voyages of exploration begun by the Portuguese in the 15th century, a distinctive type of ship had been employed. In the beginning of these voyages the Portuguese had tried "barcas", "barineles", "fustas" and "urcas" (a miscellaneous lot of sailing vessel and galley types), but had soon settled upon the caravel

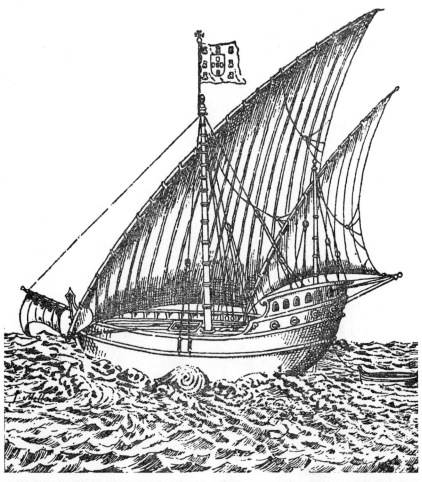

Artistic interpretation by Joaquim Melo of a caravel in a painting at the "Convento da Madre de Deus ("Convent of the Mother of God"), Lisbon, sixteenth century.

as the best exploring ship type. This class of vessel remained popular until the Cape of Good Hope had been rounded by the Portuguese navigators.

The caravel had a light-displacement hull, low-sided and sharp-ended, that fitted the capabilities of the lateen rig usually given the type in its early development. The result was a vessel that was fast and that could work to windward very well. The type name was possibly derived from the Moorish *carabo,* mentioned by San Isidoro: *Caravus parva schapha ex vime facta quae contecta crudo corio genis navigiy probet.* Also, in the Chronicles of King Alfonso XI of Castile, it is stated that, in the fleets of the Moors of Granada, Tunis and Bujia, united at Albohacen in 1339, there were galleys and ships, many of them built by the Moors and called *caravos.* (Francisco Rico, Madrid, 1787).

Lateen caravels and ship (right) in the harbour of Valenca do Minho, at the beginning of the sixteenth century, in Duarte Darmas', "Livro das Fortalezas de El-Rei D. Manuel".

Ethnologically, caravel (*caravela or carabela*) is the diminutive of *caravo,* as *galeota* is the diminutive of *galea* or *galera.* This was pointed out by Lopes de Mendonca, even though he was to suggest later, in a rather illogical comment, that the name could be a corruption of the two words *carabo a vela* (carabo under sail).

This was an error similar to the one made by Jal in his *Memoires de Archeologie Navale* when, in a flight of imagination, he assembled a word by putting together *cara* and *vela,* on the grounds that this type of vessel, viewed from forward was beautiful! (*Cara* is face; *bella*, pretty or beautiful.) Later on, in the *Glossaire Nautique*, following the ethnology suggested by Du Cange (*Glossarium ad scriptores mediae et in infimae latinitatis*, Paris, 1733) he referred to an origin, in the low Latin word *carabus*, or the Greek word *Kapapos*, applied to a ship of small dimensions.

The typical caravel of the first epoch of the Portuguese exploration period was of 50 to 60 *toneles* (1 tonel equal to 5/6 of a register ton), 20 to 25 meters long, with two or three masts fitted with lateen sails. There was neither bowsprit nor foremast, the mainmast was placed amidships and carried a lateen yard of a

Square caravel sailing in the approaches of Azores Islands, in Abraham Ortelius', "Theatrum Orbis Terrarum", 1570.

length equal to that of the hull. These vessels were developments of small fishing caravels of Portugal, mentioned in the *Foral de Vila Nova de Gaia* (1255) : *"quod piscatores dent maiordomo de unaquaque caravela unam piscem"* .... *"quod dent maiordomo decem pissotas et de unaquaque caravela siuve navigio"* ... *"et caravela extranea qui intrauerit per focem de Porti eum merca-turis."* Also, in the *Foral,* or Grant of Rights, given by the King D. Deniz to the fishermen of Paredes in the Foz de Liz, fishing caravels are mentioned (Quirino da Fonseca *A Caravela Portu-guesa,* Coimbra, 1934).

In the 15th century the Portuguese had improved the fish-ing caravel as a result of their experience with it in exploration of the west coast of Africa. Masters in the arts of its design, con-struction and handling, the Portuguese jealously concealed all information relating to the type. In spite of this, however, the seamen and shipbuilders of lower Andalusia were familiar with both the Portuguese fishing type and the improved exploration type, due to opportunities for careful examination of the vessels visiting their ports.

In order to discourage foreign interest in exploration, the Portuguese not only kept the caravel as secret as possible, but also spread the rumor that only caravels could be used for voyages of exploration on the African coast. Round ships or other types, they said, could not possibly make the round voyage, even if they suc-ceeded in reaching Guinea outward bound.

For example, Diego de Azambuja had left Lisbon December 12, 1481, with an expedition which included men who were to become famous later — such as Bartolomeu Dias and Joao Afonso de Aveiro. This expedition contained ninety caravels and two urcas or doggers (a round ship type or burdensome type of vessel) for transport under the orders of Pedro de Evora, and was to join a squadron south of Cape Verde, in the Bay of Bezeguiche, with the urcas, of 400 tons each, loaded with artillery, stone and tim-ber for the construction of a fortress at Mina. Once the cargo was unloaded, the urcas were destroyed by their crews in order to confirm the rumor that such vessels could not make the round voyage and that only caravels could.

With reference to this same matter, there is the story that during a luncheon the King of Portugal said casually that if a round ship should attempt voyages similar to those of the caravels, she would never come home. On hearing this, the distinguished pilot, Pero de Alenquer stated that he was certain he could make a round voyage with any good type and size of ship. The King immediately took exception to this, referring to the two urcas that did not come back from Mina. When Alenquer insisted it

COLUMBUS' SHIPS

could be done, the King ended the discussion by quoting a pro-
verb indicating that the pilot had merely been boasting.

However, after the luncheon the King called the pilot before
him privately, and told Alenquer that he was right but must be
silent for the good of the King's service. (*Chronica dos valerosos
e insignes feitos del Rey Dom Joham III,* by Garcia Resende, Cap.
CL, Coimbra 1798.)

Square caravel according to the measures in "Livro Nautico," at the end of
sixteenth century. From Quirino da Fonseca's "A Caravela Portuguesa".

Compared to the naos the caravels were of greater propor-
tionate length to beam. The proportion used in *naos* was 1 to 3,
but in the caravels it was 1 to 3.3. The typical caravel differed also
in that she had no raised forecastle. This was because a raised
forecastle would interfere with the necessary movement of the
heel of the main lateen yard. In the 15th century the caravels
carried lateen sails on all masts as a rule. However, they carried
a small squaresail on the main when the wind was astern. In Portugal, the lateen-rigged caravel existed longest. Quirino da Fonseca in *A Caravela Portugesa* (page 177), said that until the end of
the 15th century, the references to caravels in Portuguese documents, did not mention the kind of sail — i.e., if lateen or square

— because up to the end of the century only the lateen rig was used, there then being no Portuguese square-rigged caravels (carabela redonda) or "round caravels."

Later on, as a result of experience acquired in long ocean voyages, particularly because of the dangerous behavior of the lateen sail and yard in strong winds, the Portuguese adopted the square foresail, creating the *carabela redonda,* in imitation of some existing Spanish caravels. (The *Pinta* had been altered to a "round caravel" before leaving Palos and Columbus changed the *Nina*'s rig at the Canaries.)

This type of "round caravel" reached 180 tons in Portugal and had a foremast, which carried only square sails. The *Pinta* and *Nina,* as round caravels, carried squaresails on both fore and main masts.

The "round caravel" was also known as the *"Carabela de Armada"* (Naval Caravels), as these vessels, according to some authorities, were not only owned by the State but also caravels employed as men-of-war were rigged with square sails. Some documents refer to the *carabela redonda* as "of the Andalusian style."

Quirino da Fonseca and Admiral Gago Couninho had a controversy over the method employed to tack caravels. Fonseca maintained caravels tacked by coming about in the usual manner, but Couninho was of a contrary opinion, holding that the caravel wore around, the wind passing over the leach of the sails, in a jibe. Though Fonseca demonstrated profound knowledge of the caravels in his argument, his opponent seems to have the advantage. The Arab baggala (or "dhow"), the existing type most similar to the caravel, always wears around in a jibe, working to windward, rather than tacking.

Fernandez Duro refused to accept the caravel as a distinctive type and obstinately insisted that the name meant nothing more than a small vessel, having some features making it suited for discovery voyages. He rejected the reference to them in *Las Partidas,* though in an edition of such trustworthiness as the one by Gregorio Lopez, edited by Berni y Catala in 1767 and published in Valencia by Montfort, we find in Partida II, Titulo XXIII, Ley 7, this definite evidence: ". . . and they are listed by type names in order that they may be known, such as carraca, nao, galea, fusta, balener, leno, pinaca, carauela and other vessels." Guillen followed Fernandez Duro in this mistake, as can be seen in the former's book, *La Carabela Santa Maria*, but corrected the error in his *Historia Maritima Espanola* (1961). Quirino da Fonseca fell into this same error.

Ships in Pizigani chart (1367), at Royal Library of Parma. This is the first chart with illustrations of ships.

There are innumerable references in Spanish sources; in the letters to the residents of Palos, demanding that they contribute two caravels to the expedition; in the Columbus journal; and in the statements of such authors as Las Casas, Fernando Colon, Fernandez de Oviedo, Andres Bernaldez, Pedro Martir de Angheria, Lopez Gomara and others: *"With regard to the naos, galeras, etc., in which the voyage to England is to be made"* (MS. Urbin A, 829, page 662 Bible Vat.) "There on the coast of Spain, from Malaga to Ayamonte (are) decked caravels, barks and fishing shallops of 50 to 80 tons each." In *Servicios de los Capitanes Nodales* (Madrid, 1622), "Finding at Cape Finisterre a large ship and a caravel with British crews, fought with them."

Crescentio, in his *Nautica Mediterranea,* proposed, in 1607, the alteration of galleons (a type of ship then employed in Italy) into caravels. In this proposal he states that caravels were a specific type of vessel employed by the King of Portugal to convoy the Indies ships, guarding them from attacks by corsairs. He also states that these caravels were small ships, with four masts, besides a bowsprit, and that the foremast carries two square sails, with lateens on the other three masts. (This was the distinctive rig of the Portuguese caravels of the 16th century.) With this rig "they sail to windward, as well as the tartanes do in our waters." This emphasizes the outstanding quality of the caravel, its ability to work to windward.

The caravel has been the subject of mistakes and misinterpretations in the past, and still is. Sauvage, in a note in Book VIII, Chapter 1, *Memoires Commynes,* described caravels as seagoing vessels having oars and sails, a description more appropriate to the galleos. The caravels worked primarily under sail; if oars were used these were only employed on special occasions, to aid in turning, maneuvering in a harbor, or stemming a current. Even in these situations they could probably be handled better by being towed by a rowboat.

Monleon, who did not consider the caravel to be a distinctive type of vessel, attributed its origin to the Italians or French! Constancio assumed caravel (carabela) to have been the result of the joining of two French words, *carre* and *voile,* i.e., square-sail. However, this author also described the caravel as a vessel with lateen sails, thus contradicting himself. Another author, Rafael Bluteau, in *Glossario* (1712 ed.), describes the caravel as a "round ship using lateen sails." This is misleading, for the caravel hull was relatively long and narrow, and the distinction between the "round caravel" and the "lateen caravel" was in rigging, not in hull form. The name caravel was sometimes loosely employed. The Turks had a "caravel" that was high-sided, ornate and ungraceful in design and construction. The regency of Tunis applied the name to a ship of about 300 tons, square-rigged and carrying about 40 guns. In Normandy caravels were, at one time, a type of fishing boat — *caravella* or *crevella pescereccia,* according to the *Vocabulario di marine,* Milan, 1810, by Stratico. These were 12 to 13 meters in length overall, 4 meters in extreme breadth, with a very low freeboard. They had two masts, the main with a square course and topsail, the mizzen mast with square topsail and lateen spanker, and a bowsprit carrying headsails. They were of about 25 tons and, due to their seaworthiness and handiness, they were able to perform long voyages.

The sunset of the caravel was in the last half of the 16th century and the type disappeared, as a distinctive model and rig, early in the 17th century.

The last document known that mentions the type in Spain is of January, 1639, and it refers to a petition to the king concerning the sinking of a caravel by Tomas de Ibio Calderon. In Portugal, however, the caravel type lasted longer; the last reference known is in the *Gazeta de Lisboa,* of June 11, 1738, concerning a caravel

Ship in the manuscript of naval architecture (1445) in the British Museum.

that was driven ashore on the beach at Esmoriz while being chased by an argeline ship.

X. *THE NAOS*

In general, *nao* means ship, vessel or craft, but in Spain the *nao* was a well-defined type of merchant ship, of high freeboard, and propelled entirely by sails. This was the case later, where *navio* was the general term for the more modern *buque* or *barco* (ship). In the 18th century *navio* also was the type name of a war vessel having three masts with square sails on fore and main and a lateen, later a gaff, sail on the mizzen mast, carrying 60 or more guns — a ship-of-the-line. In this era the rigs of a *navio* and *fregata* were the same; the last was a naval ship and was distinctive because of its armament; its dimensions were smaller than those of a *navio*.

At the beginning of the Middle Ages the *nao* had but one mast, placed about amidships with a yard nearly the length of the hull on the keel, with a large sail bent to it. Ignorance of the fact that in this period *eslora* meant length on the keel, rather than overall, led many scholars to believe that these *naos* were so short and wide as to be only twice the beam in overall length. But, in reality, the old rule of one-two-three was then predominant, as remained the case during several centuries in the West, and this formula fixed the extreme breadth on the keel; while the length on deck was determined by the rule: for each unit of breadth, there were two for keel length and three for length on deck. In decked ships the depth of hold was taken as about half the beam; the same rule of *as, dos, tres,* would also apply for establishing the depth of hold in relation to beam and keel length. The selected proportions were used for a long period, as can be seen by Thome Cano's statement in his *Arte para fabricar, fortificar y aparejar naos de guerra y merchantes,* Sevilla, 1611—"The master builders of Spain, Italy and of other nations that built *naos* are of the habit of employing one cubit of extreme breadth, two of keel with one added to give three for total length; using one for width of floor in three cubits of breadth and making the depth of hull about three-quarters of the extreme breadth, without utilizing the other measurements." Even in the first half of the 19th century the proportion of beam to length was not over four. In galleys, the proportion was length of eight, or even ten, times the beam; in *galeotas* and *bergantines* (small galleys) it was about five.

In the earliest *naos* of which pictures exist, the bow and stern were nearly alike, with full ends, each having "castles" for war purposes. On the mast head there was a fighting top or crow's nest, to be used for a lookout and, particularly, as a suitable place in combat for several slingers or archers.

The appearance of the axial or pivoted rudder attached to a straight sternpost brought about a change in the shape of the ends of the hull, a difference that became more apparent as the afterbody or run was made sharper to give a better flow of water to the rudder blade that was necessary for good steering qualities. *The rounded form at the stern, above water, made by curving the planking up to the bottom of the transom or flat upper stern, characteristic of the naos, continued into later centuries, producing what was later called, in English, the "round tuck."** The early axial rudder had appeared, as far as pictorial evidence goes, in the seal of the English city of Ipswich sometime after the year 1200. The rudder is shown in the seal supported by pintles and gudgeons. Another example may be in a ship carved of marble on the font in the Cathedral of Winchester, of 1180, and probably made in Belgium. Laird Clowes states that a careful examination of this had convinced him that what appears to be a rudder is actually a large steering oar, more vertical than usual. In any case, it can be said that the axial rudder, attached to a vertical sternpost, came into use sometime about the end of the 12th century, or early in the 13th century, in substitution for the two large steering oars in Mediterranean vessels or the one oar used in the north of Europe. In the northern European vessels the single oar, by custom, was on the starboard side of the hull (in Anglo-Saxon *steorboard* (*steor = rudder, bord = side.*) The opposite side of the hull, the *port* side, received its name because, in ancient times, this side of the vessel, being free of the obstruction of the steering oar, was the one always tied to a pier in harbor.

There were distinct differences in shipbuilding practices between the Mediterranean and the north of Europe. In the Mediterranean the planking of the hull was finished smooth at the seams (or *caravel planked*, in English). In northern Europe *lap strake* was employed in which the planking lapped at each seam; the upper strake or plank always overriding, or lapping, the upper edge of the strake below for a short depth. This was also known as *clench* or *clinker* planking. In large vessels, experience showed that the smooth *caravel* planking system gave the better results, though *lap strake* planking has remained popular in small craft, such as lifeboats, as it is a light and flexible system of construction.

In the Mediterranean area the two earliest representations of medieval ships known are in two Greek manuscripts of the end of the 9th century — one now in Paris and the other in Moscow.

*Editor's annotation.

These show the triangular lateen sail, as it was called by North European seamen when they had become acquainted with the rig of vessels of the Latin countries. However, the sail did not originate in the Mediterranean area but was brought in by the Arabs of the Red Sea, who probably received the sail-form from the Pacific at some early period.

The square sail, employed by the seamen of ancient Egypt, and used by the Greeks and Romans, did not disappear entirely from the Mediterranean in medieval times, but until the middle of the 14th century it was not widely used there; the lateen having replaced it in popularity. In the period when the axial or hinged rudder was introduced from northern Europe, the square sail again came into widespread use. This sail form, in Spanish, was confusingly named the "round sail". In fact, it was neither "square" nor "round," but rectangular in shape. In ships of the Atlantic coast of Europe, the lateen would remain in use only as a mizzen sail or spanker until late in the 18th century. The change from lateen to gaff, in ships' spankers, was ordered in Spain in 1785, but some ships-of-the-line carried the lateen spanker yard as late as Trafalgar.

Good examples of lateen naos of the Mediterranean were those of the King St. Louis, used in the crusade in 1268. There ships were the Venetian *Rocheforte* and the Genovese ship, name unknown, but referred to as *Nao X* when described by Jal. The *Rocheforte* was 36 meters long, 23 meters length of keel, 13.3 meters extreme beam and 12.9 meters depth in hold. The fore and after bodies were very full and nearly alike. The hull had two flush decks from end to end. The lower hold, below the first or lower deck and the bottom, was employed for stowage of food, ammunition and heavy cargo. The 'tween decks was employed for the transport of the knights' horses; the upper deck reached from side to side only under the "castles" at bow and stern; in the waist it was no more than two gangways along the sides of 2 or 2.5 meters width each, there being a large opening or hatch between the gangways. These gangways, besides being passageways connecting the castles, were used by archers in battle, sheltering themselves under the bulwarks which were about 1.5 meters high. The ship's boat was stowed over the hatchway between the gangways, a practice that continued through the 18th century. The castles might have two or three decks, the after castle was often round and formed a combat area (*bellatorium*) that also seved as a place for relaxation for persons quartered in that elevated part of the nao. Over this there was sometimes an awning fitted, as in the galleys (*tendal*).

In order to have a knowledge of the rig of the naos, it is necessary to examine the *Nao X* because the *Rocheforte* painting does not show this. In the Genovese ship the larger mast was the one forward — of 25 meters length, about 1 meter in diameter, located with its heel at the bottom of the curved stempost where it meets the keel. The aftermast, of 23 meters length, was placed a little abaft mid-length on the keel. On each mast there was a lateen sail, the yards were 31 and 27 meters in length, respectively.

As has been indicated, the lateen rigged *naos,* seen only in the Mediterranean, eventually disappeared, replaced by the *round naos.* The latter at first had one mast, then was given two. These carried a single sail on each mast; in the two-masted *naos* there was one large square sail on the foremast and a lateen mizzen. The two-masted *nao* is shown for the first time in the atlas of Pizigani of 1367 and this type was also confined almost entirely to the Mediterranean. A magnificent example is the model of a *nao* of 1450 which was formerly in the chapel of San Simon, at Mataro (Barcelona) and now in the Maritiem Museum Prins Hendrik at Rotterdam. Another example is the nao represented in the altar piece *"Episodio de la vida de Santa Ursula,"* the work of Juan de Reixach, 1468, that originally was in the church of Cubells (Lerida) and is now in the Art Museum of Catalonia, Barcelona.

The great importance of the nao model of Mataro, mysteriously taken out of Spain, is that its builder obviously was not ignorant of ships and shipbuilding and it is the only three dimensional representation of a ship of the Middle Ages. The next contemporary model of a ship is over a hundred years later, while of earlier models there is naught but the models of river craft found in the tombs of the Egyptian pharaohs.

In the north of Europe, the two-masted naos were not employed. In order to obtain better balance in rig in the nao, however, they adopted a three-masted sail plan. A manuscript of Lord Hastings, attributed by some to have been written about 1450, shows a three masted nao, but this is questionable and it is very doubtful that a three-masted rig, like this, existed. The earliest document that we have is the seal of Louis de Bourbon which may be dated precisely as of 1466; this shows a nao of three masts and may be the earliest graphic representation of the type. Two graffitos in brick in the Carmelitan nunnery of Helsingor, show ships of three and four masts, which are supposedly of 1430. (*Segel Och Motor,* Carl Solver, Stockholm, 1936, No. 8).

In 1492 the nao was a distinctive type of sailing ship, strongly built and formed by the traditional formula (*as-dos-tres*) 1-2-3. In Spain, 1 = extreme breadth, 2 = keel length, 3 = length on deck. The nao, in 1492, had castles at bow and stern; she was square-rigged on the main and fore mast, with a bowsprit having a sprit sail, a lateen on the mizzen mast and, in some vessels, a topsail over the fighting top on the main mast, the only top carried, as at this date there was no fighting-top on the foremast. This produced a hull and rig combination in which a burdensome vessel and powerful rig was obtained. Slower and more cumbersome than the caravel, and also less weatherly, the nao then ranged between 100 and 200 tons burden, much less than the famous carracks which, with similar hull-form and rig, ranged upward to 600 tons burden in the large vessels of the type employed between Mediterranean ports and those of the Hanseatic League and Britain. In Spain, even though the large carracks were not in use, the term (from the Latin *carica,* cargo) had appeared in the *Cronica de Pero Nino* in 1405.

Northern methods of construction were introduced into the Mediterranean in 1304, according to the Florentine historian Villani, who died in 1348: "In this period some North Europeans, from Bayonne in Gascony, passed through the Strait of Sevilla (sic) — (really Strait of Gibraltar) with ships called *cogs,* with which they engaged in piracy in the Mediterranean and did great damage. Since then, Genovese, Venetians and Catalonians have adopted the *cog* and have abandoned the use of large ships in order to carry out voyages with more certainty and more economically." By then the characteristics of the North European *cog* were: clinker, or lap-strake, hull, square sail rig with vertical mast, crow's nest round and low, raking straight stem, with nearly equal sheer fore and aft (with perhaps a little more sheer fore than aft), straight raking sternpost with hinged rudder attached and large castles at bow and stern, for working the bowlines of the square mainsail; the Hanseatic cogs had reef-points. Most of these features do not appear to have been adopted by Mediter-

ranean shipbuilders until their adoption of the cog design in some
degree.

The Mediterranean *naos* were then marked by having caravel-
planked hulls, mast raked forward and a single large lateen sail.
Two oars, one on each side, and protected by quarter galleries,
were employed for steering. The sheer was greatest aft, the bow
relatively low, and with a small castle. The stern had little or no
rake. The fighting top was an elongated basket in form, placed
abaft the mast head.

Near the end of the 15th century new features had developed
in North Europe; reef points came into wide use; castles became
part of the hull itself rather than mere superstructure; the yard
was in one piece and shrouds were attached to the mast inside the
fighting top, or at the trestle trees. The tye of the mainyard had
its upper block below the trestle trees. The shrouds were fitted
over channels with chain plates, ratlines, lanyards, and deadeyes.

On the Mediterranean some new ideas appeared also: bonnets
were fitted to sails, lateen and square sail yards were made of
two pieces, shrouds were secured to the mast under the crow's
nest. Sheaves for the tyes of the mainyard were brought up inside
the fighting top or at the doubling. Shrouds without ratlines were
set up at the rail or planksheer with tackles. A rope ladder on the
afterside of the masts was used. In the hull, the ends of the deck
beams extended through the planking and out from the sides a
little.

By this time, the characteristics of rig and construction of ships
of Northern and Southern Europe were becoming rapidly similar
and the nao that developed showed a trend toward the galleon
and navio of the next century. This trend, in the 18th century,
produced the sailing ship of the great naval powers and, before sail
finally went out of use, the splendid clipper ship was developed in
which sail propulsion reached the highest level of efficiency, sur-
passed only in the modern yacht rig of the jib-headed types in some
respects, due to the accumulated knowledge obtained by aero-
nautic and hydrodynamic research.

PART II

The New Reconstruction

XI. *THE SANTA MARIA WAS A NAO*

I N ALL the reconstructions of the *Santa Maria* (except Guillen's of 1929, reproduced in 1951) the type of ship to which she belonged has been carefully studied and it has been generally accepted that the flagship of Columbus' squadron on his first voyage was a nao. This is the conclusion of scholarly historians and of informed marine archeologists of various nationalities, who recently have made extensive examination of the matter. Among these are Anderson, Ballesteros, Fonseca, Landstrom, Morison and Winter. This conclusion has become so well established, in fact, that the majority of authorities accept it without question, though they often support their acceptance with only casual evidence as a result.

In Spain, however, there has been a popular idea that the *Santa Maria* was a caravel, in opposition to the old, accepted decision that the vessel was a nao — even though that decision was first reached by Fernandez-Duro, a Spaniard. It is therefore desirable to discuss here the long-established evidence, as well as some new, that has come to light.

The proposition that the *Santa Maria* was a nao and not a caravel is based on these facts:

1. Columbus, commonly precise in naming ship types, called the *Santa Maria* a *nao* eighty-one times in his journal, even though the flagship did not make the complete round voyage, having been wrecked in the West Indies during the first voyage of Columbus. Only twice is the vessel referred to as a caravel — in abbreviated passages, probably inserts of the transcriber, as for example, a reference to "the three caravels" (Aug. 8 and Sept. 6, 1492).

The false assumption that the Santa Maria was a caravel is founded on such references, disregarding the eighty-one references by Columbus himself in the journal. There are references, obviously in loose writing, such as the orders of the King for the preparation of *Tres carabelas de Armada* (three naval caravels) for the use of Columbus. The lack of technical precision in the official correspondence of this period is emphasized by reference to another order, in which not "three caravels" are mentioned but *tres fustas de Armada* (three naval fustas). Now, *fustas* were small galleys, so a literal translation of the order could only be taken as a joke.

2. The precision of language used by Columbus is interesting — when he is referring to three ships together he calls them *navios,* but individually he refers to them as *nao* or *caravel.* In no case does he call a caravel a nao, or the nao a caravel, when referring to them individually.

3. It is impossible to accept the position taken by Jal, first, and repeated later by Alcala Galiano and Guillen, who all argue that when Columbus uses nao he refers to the nao-capitana, flagship, of the squadron instead of to a definite type of carrack because, in that case, after the wreck of the *Santa Maria,* when Columbus transferred his flag to the *Nina,* he would continue to call her a nao. But actually he called the *Nina,* without exception, a caravel throughout the journal. There are in fact ninety-seven instances where the *Nina* and *Pinta* are called caravels, in Columbus' journal during the round voyage.

4. There have been very few authors — only one is actually known to me — that presume the *Santa Maria* to be a caravel. Guillen offers as proof of this the fact the Spanish tradition refers to "three caravels." The tradition, if there be one, is among the many absurd fabrications. It would be the result of convenience, for it is easier to say "three caravels" than "a nao and two cara-

vels." Tradition is always lacking in technical precision, especially with reference to the sea and its navigation.

There was also the reputation and fame of the caravels used in the Portuguese discoveries, as well as by Columbus, just as all modern square-rigged ships are now called "clippers" by the press and public in America. Internationally, regulations applying to "steamers" are legally and popularly assumed to include all the powered vessels or motor-ships. A similarly loose treatment of the rig of yachts is found in the press, due to the fact that all of these careless applications of precise technical marine terms are by land-lubbers, who confuse sloop with cutter, ketch with yawl and the like.

5. A careful reading of the Columbus' journal will suggest, to persons acquainted with sailing, that the *Santa Maria* was an entirely different type of vessel than the *Pinta* and *Nina*. The *Santa Maria* is shown to have been heavier working, not weatherly (she could not lay up nearer than 7 points to the wind, but the caravels could sail within 5 or 5½ points of the wind.) The outstanding qualities of the caravels are shown to be their light displacement and easy handling, and their nimbleness, which were often referred to by Columbus as when he said of an Indian canoe "the canoe that is his caravel" on December 12th. It can also be seen that on a number of instances the caravels had to shorten sail in order not to lose sight of the flagship or nao capitana.

6. The rig of the *Santa Maria,* fortunately, is mentioned in the journal. This is another conclusive proof that she was a typical nao, as in all drawings and paintings of the period one cannot find a single case of a caravel that carried the five sails of the nao — four square sails and a lateen. This rig is always shown on the hull of a nao.

7. Columbus, in the numerous unabridged transcriptions, when he and not the transcriber apparently speaks (such as the entries for October 14th and October 19th) gives contrasting information on the nao and caravels.

8. Pedro Martir de Angheria, a compatriot of Columbus and a contemporary, makes a reference, in his *De Orbe Novo,* (1516) dec. 1, lib. 1, to the ships of the first voyage of discovery — *Tria nauigia: unum onerarium caueatum. Alia duo mercatoria leuia sine caueis, quae ab Hcspanis carauelae uocantur.* The meaning of *caueatum* is not *con cubierta* (with deck), as some have sup-

posed, but rather *con cofa,* "with a crow's nest or round top" —
and the *Santa Maria* alone carried a crow's nest.

The above-mentioned error in translation led to another mistaken but popular conception — that the caravels *Nina* and *Pinta*
were open, undecked vessels. This is, of course, a proven error and
the heavy gales that the two caravels weathered on their home-
ward voyage proved their seaworthiness and sailing ability. In
summing up, all known references about Columbus' ships agree
with Pedro Martir — "Three ships, one of burden having a crow's
nest, the other two merchantmen without crow's nests that Spaniards call caravels."

A and B: single masted ships painted in miniature by Domingo de Adanar
in the Codex "Les bones costumes e els bons usatges de la mar" ("The good
habitudes and the good usages of the Sea"), in the Municipal Archives of
Valencia. — C and D: ships in a tapestry of the cathedral of Zamora (fifteenth
century). Notice the parrel of the main yard and rope for hauling weapons
and missiles to the crow's nest on the mast midships (D) in the vessel without
forecastle (like the caravels of this time).

9. The *Santa Maria* had the nao's characteristic forecastle, as
is shown by the journal, October 14th, "at 10 o'clock at night,
being on the stern castle I saw a light . . . prayed, and insisted that

a good watch be kept on the *forecastle*." The caravels, on the contrary, did not have a raised forecastle, for such a structure would interfere with the handling of the tack of the lateen; the *Nina* was entirely lateen rigged when leaving Palos. The *Pinta,* converted from a lateener to carry square sails on the main mast before the beginning of the voyage, may have had a slightly raised deck or grating forward. But there does not appear to have been time to add a forecastle and it is probable such an addition would have unbalanced the vessel, as she must have been quite sharp forward. Such a vessel could be overloaded forward if much weight were added there.

10. The *Santa Maria* is commonly supposed to have been built in the Cantabric, in either Galicia or Santander, where there was no construction of the caravel type. The Galician origin of the vessel is indicated by her name at the time she was chartered by Columbus for his first voyage, *La Gallega* (the *Galician*). If she were a Montañesa from Santander, there is only the local tradition that she was built at Colindres (Province of Santander) to support the assertion.

Everything stated heretofore combines to give support to the theory that the *Santa Maria* was a nao, with very little and doubtful support to the theory that she was some kind of a caravel. Therefore, the new reconstruction of the *Santa Maria* will show a conception of what a typical nao was in hull, rig and fittings, at the end of the 15th century, in Spain.

XII. *PRINCIPAL DIMENSIONS*

Once the type of vessel to which the *Santa Maria* belonged can be reasonably established, it is necessary to decide upon her dimensions. It has been pointed out that Jal, Fernandez Duro and Guillen had deduced her dimensions from an assumed length of a ship's boat, based upon an erroneous interpretation of a passage in Columbus' journal.

D'Albertis, however, based his dimensions upon the then assumed crew requirement of forty men (an estimate of the men on board now accepted generally) though he arrived at his crew size on the work of an author, Escalante, who wrote almost a century after Columbus. After such a passage of time, the methods of construction and rigging had notably changed. Albertis' plans, therefore, showed an extremely large ship, since the forty-man "crew" taken on this voyage was, in fact, abnormal for a nao of the tonnage of the *Santa Maria* in Columbus' time. In short, the requirements of Columbus were really due to imagined conditions he expected to meet in the "Indies," rather than to the simple needs of navigation, or of economics.

After much study of so important a matter, it was decided to try to base the dimensions of the nao only on her tonnage; she was said to be of little over 100 tons burthen. To do this required the forming of a floating vessel that would give the specified hold capacity and that would also be within the proportions that were characteristic of the Spanish naos of the period.

In 1492 a ship's tonnage was an estimate of the number of wine barrels, or *tuns,* that she could carry, a tun being taken as two *pipes* of wine. This was an ancient mode of measurement, going back to Greek and Roman ships, in which cargo capacity was measured in *amphorae,* a Greek *amphora* had usually a capacity of about 38 liters, while a Roman *amphora* was of 25 liters. The tribune of the plebes, Flaminino Nepos, restricted Roman ships in 232 B.C. to a capacity of 300 *amphorae,* if they were owned by senators, showing the Roman mode of tonnage then in use.

Quirino da Fonseca, who was an authority on this subject, states that the Sevelle tun, of two pipes, or of eight cubic cubits, was of 1.405 cubic meters. Other writers give slightly different equivalents. Columbus, in 1494, proposed the adoption of the Seville tun as the standard unit and referred to *arqueo* which was a measurement of the capacity of the pipes of wine. There was another measurement in use in Spain; the *tonel macho* or Biscay tun which was larger than the Seville tun — ten Biscay tuns equalled twelve Seville tuns, and a Biscay tun equalled 1.683 cubic meters.

The Seville tun is taken as the probable unit because of Columbus' known preference. The number of these to be assigned to the new reconstruction was then examined. Padre Las Casas, in his *Historia de las Indies,* states only that the nao was somewhat larger than Columbus' other ships. His extracts of the third voyage, however, refers to the nao used by Columbus as of around 100 tons. Columbus' son, Ferdinand, in his *Historia della vita e de fatti dell' Ammiraglio D. Christoforo Columbo,* Venice, 1571, gives 110 tons as the burthen of this nao with the added information that she drew three Genoese fathoms, equivalent to 5.71 feet.

Escalante de Mendoza, in his *Itinerario de la navegacion por los mares y tierras occidentales,* 1585, states the tonnage of Columbus' ships. (The publication of this book was not approved by the Indies Council [Consejo de Indias] because it was feared at that time that the information collected by the author in his 28 years at sea could fall into enemies' hands.) This author says, "Don Cristobal Colon, who discovered and initiated the navigation of the Occidental Indies, did not choose or look for large ships for his great venture but for very small ones, just a little over 100 tuns." It is not possible to identify the source of his statement. In view of Columbus' remarks on the unhandiness of the *Santa Maria,* it is very unlikely that he would desire a larger nao in subsequent voyages of discovery.

Tentatively accepting "a little over 100 tons" as a measure of capacity, the hull dimensions were determined in the following manner — trial-and-error dimensions of beam, keel and length, on the one-two-three ratio with a depth in hold in proportion to the beam, were employed to calculate a capacity and structure that would produce 100 tons burthen. Once these dimensions were determined, a half-model was made, with due regard to the appearance and probable form of naos built before 1492.

In order to decide the profile of the rabbets and rake of ends, sheer and crown of main deck, the Mataro model was referred to; the buttocks and run were based upon the nao on an altar by Juan de Reixach and that in the painting *The Pilgrimage of Breydenbach.* The bow was based upon the naos shown in Benincasa's chart and Carpaccio's great paintings. The Venetian artist best known for the carrack signed *WA,* (Winter believes that the *W* is the sole initial and the apparent *A* to be a mark) was also referred to and the nao in the Barcelonese edition of 1502, of the *Libre del Consolat dels Maritims,* was used for sheering and profile details (forecastle, waist, upper deck, poop and round house).

The half-model was used in this study; the sections were altered as knowledge of the form of the hull developed. Care was taken to keep to the correct proportions. Then the working drawing of the lines from the half-model proceeded, with further adjustments in both model and drawing. When all alterations and adjustments were made, a new calculation showed the capacity to be 105.97 tuns. This being considered acceptable, and after de-

Ship in the chart of Grazioso Benincasa, 1482 in the Library of Bologna University. Note the following items. Small foremast, mainsail with square reinforcers, bonnet and central sheet, topsail, topmast with shrouds, bowlines of the mainsail running by the bowsprit, frames turning inside, double halliard, raised poop, clinker planking in the forecastle, and as an exception, woodlings on the mizzen-mast.

signing the rig and estimating the weight of structure, spars, rigging, armament, fittings, stores, the displacement was established and the draft verified; stability calculations were also made. With all of this completed, the final plans were drawn and two scale models built.

The characteristics of this version of the *Santa Maria* are: Beam, 7.92 meters; keel length, 15.8 meters; deck length, 23.6 meters; depth in hold, 3.85 meters; draft, light 2.1 meters; height of mainmast to topmast, 26.6 meters; length of mainyard, 16.4 meters; and burthen 105.9 tuns.

THE NEW RECONSTRUCTION

In this attempted reconstruction of a 100 tun nao, the hull-form and design characteristics of the period of 1492 were interpreted from the best graphic material available, showing the common features of the type rather than an individual and possibly an unusual vessel. A typical nao of the period would also give a better impression of the age of Columbus to the intelligent viewer than would a possibly abnormal vessel.

Naturally, in the selection of graphics and documentary evidence, preference was given to material of Spanish origin, since the nao was Spanish-built.

Carrack in "Regimento de Estrolabio e do Quadrante", the oldest Portuguese nautical book known at present (about 1510). The only copy is in the Staatbibliothek Munchen.

COLUMBUS' SHIPS

It is unnecessary to dwell upon the fact that no plans, drawings or other graphic material can be accepted as representing the *Santa Maria.* The well-known picture of a nao in *Oceania Classis,* shown on the Columbus chart of 1493, was partially rejected because it is a copy of the one in the *Peregrinacion de Breydenbach,* (*The Pilgrimage of Breydenbach*), 1486, off Modon, (now Mothoni) port of call of pilgrims on the southwest coast of Greece, to which had been added the title *Oceanica Classis.*

However, the knowledge of shipbuilding of the period that is indicated made it a somewhat useful reference for hull-form, upperworks and rigging.

Little importance was placed on the chart of Hispaniola in the Biblioteca Colombina and attributed carelessly to Bartolomé Colon, because it cannot be connected to the first voyage, as D'Albertis has pointed out. The chart was drawn about 1530 and it is noticeable that the larger of the ships does not carry a spritsail as did the *Santa Maria.* The artist of the period always showed ships under full sail, so it is unlikely the draftsman was trying to show the vessel with this sail furled.

To clarify the matter further, the naos shown have all the characteristics of the 16th century rather than of the 15th, and Columbus did not have a vessel rigged entirely as a lateener, since *Nina* had been transformed into a square rigger at the Canaries before he reached the West Indies.

The nao and the Castilian caravel, together with seven Portuguese vessels shown in Juan de la Cosa's chart of 1501, are too poorly drawn to deduce detail and the nao and the Castilian caravel are shown off the Brazilian coast, which Columbus did not visit or see on his first voyage.

XIII. *ORIGIN OF THE NAME OF THE SANTA MARIA*

On being selected by Columbus, the nao was officially named *Santa Maria.* This was done at Palos. This port had been ordered to provide two caravels for the voyage by the King and Queen. Columbus made arrangements for the nao with her owner and captain, Juan de la Cosa (a native of Santona) who was to continue on board as the master of the ship. Authorities agree that this man was not the famous cartographer of the same name — a good thing for the latter's memory, if the acts and general behav-

Portuguese carrack in chart of Juan de la Cosa.

ior of the master of the ship, when the nao was wrecked at Hispaniola, are true.

Before Columbus obtained this nao she had been known as
La Gallega, perhaps because she had been built in Galicia, as has
been steadfastly claimed. It is difficult to accept any other possibility, even though the town of Colindres (Santander) makes the
claim. In this case there is no supporting data or reasoning
offered, other than a mere local tradition. Another tradition has
the *Santa Maria* a trader to the Low Countries. No justification

Castilian carrack in chart of Juan de la Cosa.

for these theories and claims has been produced. Fernandez de Oviedo refers to her original name many times and the suggestion of the late Professor Jack (Massachusetts Institute of Technology) that *La Gallega* was merely a nickname inferring a crude, ugly and not very seaworthy ship, does not have verisimilitude, for if this ship were slow and heavy-working, compared to the caravels, she was no more awkward than the rest of her type, apparently. Columbus' complaints about this ship were about her speed, weatherliness and draft, not about her seaworthiness, rolling, or stability.

In this period it was not unusual for a ship to have an official or "register" name and a nickname, the latter generally the selection of the crew. As a result, the nickname might be used more often in a report than the official name, or vice-versa. An example of use of a nickname is *La Nina,* whose register name was the *Santa Clara,* named after the patron saint of the village of Mogeur.

The nickname was usually related to the name of the owner or captain, or place of build, or armament, or seaworthiness, or appearance, or behavior, etc. Thus, the caravel of Gonzalo Bachillev was called *La Bachillera;* another caravel used on the fourth voyage of Columbus was officially named *Santiago de Palos* and nicknamed *Bermuda* because her master was Francisco Bermudez; another built at Vizcaya, on the Cantabric, was nicknamed *Vizcaina,* and another *La Nina,* was named for her owner, Juan Nino, of Moguer. *La Pinta* was owned by Cristobal Quintero, of Palos, but may have received her nickname by having previously been owned by the Pintos, a family also from Palos.

The first Spanish vessel built in the West Indies was named *Santa Cruz* but nicknamed *La India.* Another vessel was owned by Francisco Garcia, who also was her master, and she was nicknamed *La Garza.* The speed of the caravel, used in the third voyage of Columbus, was the reason why she was called *El Correo;* and *La Gorda,* a caravel of 60 tuns in which Colon returned to Spain in 1500, was named for her owner, Andres Martin de la Gorda.

XIV. *THE HULL*

In Columbus' time it would have been very difficult to find a vessel of burthen in Spain that was any better than the *Santa Maria.* Though Columbus complained about the *Santa Maria* at the time of her loss, saying she was slow and awkward to handle, at his departure from Spain he had remarked, "I have fitted out three very able vessels for the voyage."

In reconstructing the *Santa Maria,* her full lines and strongly curved timbers required substantial longitudinals (bilge stringers, clamps and wales) as well as vertical guards for, as Garcia del Palacio was to say nearly a century later than 1492, "the vertical guards give the best support to the vessel when she is careened for repairs."

The transom stern, one-half the beam in width, was typical of Spanish naos; it rested on a cross-seam beam, slightly V in shape, with the planking coming up round and full, below the cross-seam, in a "round tuck."

The planking was, of course, smooth seam or "caravel." This name for smooth planking had been adopted in Northern Europe because it had been seen there in Spanish and Portuguese caravels. The use of the name has led to a false belief that there were English, Flemish and Scandinavian vessels of the Mediterranean caravel type in the 15th century.

Above the main rail cap forward, below the raised forecastle, the tri-angular space on each side was planked clinker, or lap-strake, as was noted to have been the fashion of the period. This was shown in the Mataro model and numerous other examples, including the nao of Benincasa. There was one peculiarity, however, for in all cases the lap was toward the bow and not toward the stern, as seamanlike common sense would seem to dictate. Lapping toward the stern would appear to produce less strain and disturbance when the vessel pitched heavily into a sea. Perhaps the lapping forward was a relic of an earlier period when lap strakes in the topsides ran around the bow more or less parallel to the sheer, or was the result of an effort to find easier construction of the very full bow. The plan of the raised forecastle deck and rail had long been a straight-sided triangle and not rounded to follow the planksheer and mainrail. In much earlier times it had been rectangular in plan — at one time it was pentagonal, as shown in the nao drawn by Gentile de Fabriano in *The Miricales of St. Nicholas* of about 1430, a type of Mediterranean vessel then having a rockered keel, with curved sternpost.

The correct fastenings to be used were treenails — wooden dowels — that remained in use until modern times. Also, some iron and copper fastenings were used, particularly in Biscay. In the reconstruction, wood and wrought iron were to be used. Ship carpenters in some parts of Spain still know how to make treenails of square wooden bars by driving these through a round cutting-edged hole in a steel tube or plate mounted on a heavy block. The resulting treenail, or dowel, will swell into its hole when driven and is a fastening of very great strength and lasting qualities.

The frames or "timbers" of the nao were in single futtocks, joined end to end and widely spaced, with double futtock floor timbers but separated from one another across the keel, and a keel-son above. The timbers were reinforced by doubled floor timbers, with a keelson above, as in the Mataro model. At the stern, cant timbers and transom timbers were used, while at the stem cants and a stem apron were used. The deadwoods were formed of heavy stuff and knees.

The deck beams were heavily crowned, the ends well secured to waterways, shelves and clamps. Under the waterways, salt stops were placed at the bottom of the clamps; salt is used as a preservative in the reconstruction as an added effect to ventilation and was not used in Columbus' time. The heavy deck crown can still be seen in the Spanish feluccas and other fishing craft and was also a feature of the galleys and some sailing-rowing Mediterranean types.

The deck beams were supported, in the hold, by rough-tree stanchions or pillars, stepped on the keelson. Those under the hatch coamings were cleated to form ladders.

One of the characteristics of ship construction in Southern Europe and the Mediterranean was the projecting beam ends, extending a short distance outboard, through the planking. The purpose of them has been a mystery to scholars, even though this peculiarity is to be seen from the time of Queen Hatshepsut, 1500 B.C. to the latter part of the 15th century. By 1530 the northern method of ending deck beams inside the planking had become dominant. The foremost projecting beam ends may have been used to attach a bridle to, in hauling the vessel ashore. One pair of projecting beam ends are still to be seen in the Turkish Black Sea fishing boats.* The purpose of the other beams is conjectural, however.

The strakes of the hull planking were to be about 10 centimeters in thickness on the wales and 8 centimeters on the rest of the planking. The seams were caulked with oakum and tar. Ceiling was not employed until later. The wales were usually rounded on the outside face, being formed of split trees with edges faired. Vertical guard timbers protected these, as shown in many pictures of naos of the period, including the Mataro model.

*Report to the Government of Turkey on Fishing Boats, by Howard I. Chapelle, N.A., FAO Report No. 706, Expanded Technical Assistance Program, Food and Agriculture Organization of the United Nations, Rome, 1957.

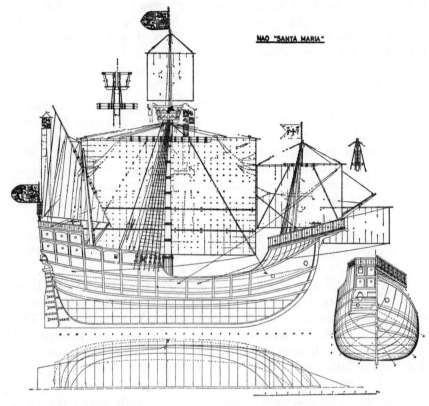

Santa Maria — Hull lines and sail plan of the Martinez-Hidalgo reconstruction (1963).

The ballast was of two types, fixed and movable. The fixed or permanent ballast was of mortar. In the reconstruction this would amount to about 25 tons weight, distributed over the bottom of the ship and to above the tops of the floors. A gutter was formed in the top of this ballast, on each side of the keelson, to carry bilge water to the pumps, located on the forward side of the midship frame. The movable ballast, put aboard when no cargo was being carried or when light or partly loaded, was sand, gravel or beach stones, stowed as required to give the necessary trim and stability. A ballast stone apparently was referred to by Columbus when, on the 4th of October 1492, he mentions a stone being thrown by a youth aboard one of the caravels and refers also to stones aboard the vessels like those used by slingers or for balls in falconets.

The midsection was formed with the greatest beam at about the height of the main deck; tumble-home had not developed because the problems of the weight of broadside armament on hull strength in the topsides had not yet appeared. Only at the raised quarterdeck and in the poop cabin sides does some tumble-home appear. The floors of the midsection show no deadrise for one-third the beam. This was to allow the vessel to ground, without excessive heel, when brought ashore for inspection and careening or repair.

The stern was round-tuck, as can be seen in practically all representations of the period. As stated earlier, the term "round tuck" means that the outer bottom plank and lower side plank turn up abruptly, near the stern, to the bottom of the transom. All of this planking ends on the vertical stern post or upon the cross-seam beam, which together form a T-shape.

Fernandez Duro and Monleon made the error of showing a square tuck stern, in which the lower planking ends upon the vertical stern post or on the sides of a flat lower transom. Only in Behaim could be seen a nao with a square stern, 1492, but that could be attributed to careless restoration many years later. It was not until the 16th century that the square-tuck stern came into general use in Spain, when it became typical of the galleons for a time, but these ships eventually returned to the round-tuck stern, which remained in use until they disappeared. However, it is correct to accept the square-tuck stern in the caravels like the *Nina* and *Pinta,* a feature which is verified by the graphic material on this type, both Spanish and Portuguese.

The rudder backing pieces were as thick as the stern-post. The shape of the rudder and of the gudgeons and pintles in the reconstruction were copied from the Carrack of WA, fitted with a tiller on the main deck to which the rudder or steering tackles could be rigged. A ring-bolt on the after edge of the rudder, almost level with the waterline, is for the rudder-pendants or preventers which lead through the fashion pieces of the transom. On the nao the helmsman could not see the sails when steering and had to depend upon the watch officer and a remarkable sensitivity to the "feel" of the tiller just as modern yachtsmen do in getting the most out of their boats in steering. It was not until the 18th century that the steering wheel, drum and steering-ropes came into use. An earlier solution was the vertical "whipstaff", introduced at the end of the 16th century. This was a staff passing through a main or upper deck opening, where it was pivoted to allow port to starboard movement. The lower end was toggled to the end of the tiller or fitted with the rudder-pendants which led to the after edge of the rudder, as indicated in the Carrack of WA, the Flemish artist. The whipstaff was worked by the helmsman standing on the deck above the tiller; sometimes the helmsman was on a raised platform on this deck, and could see the sails.

Not all helmsmen would be skillful — *battle helmsmen* is the term used by the Spanish to mark those who are highly competent. These are the steersmen employed when entering and leaving port or in dangerous waters. Those men could steer by compass-courses and by the wake seen through the rudder-port.

It should be noted that the ability to hold a straight course then as now required a proper balance of hull and sail area. In turning and working, a most important part was played by the mizzen. For "falling off" to leeward, the foresail and the bowsprit sprit-sail, and later the triangular headsail, served this purpose.

Besides the scuppers there were mooring ports in the main deck bulwarks for shore-fasts. Hawse ports, for the anchor cables, were in the bows; in the transom there were also hawse ports on each side of the rudder port. All these were leather-lined. There were small openings for the mainsail sheets at the stern, and, at the break of the forecastle, there were others for the tacks. In the waist were two for the foresheets and in the forecastle were others for the tacks and for the lanyards of the mainstay. The earliest evidence of lanyards on the Mediterranean is on the relief carvings of the tomb of San Pedro Martir, in the church of Saint Eustorgio, Milan, of the 14th century. In the bulwarks of the quarter deck there were two small rectangular ports through which the breech-loading bombards pointed. Port-covers had not come into use and these guns were fixed so there was no recoil. (See Section XVIII.) The only port with a cover in this period was a cargo port or timber port in the port side of the stern of the nao of Juan de Reixach.

The main deck has three feet of sheer in its whole length; amidships is a large cargo hatch of such dimensions as will pass

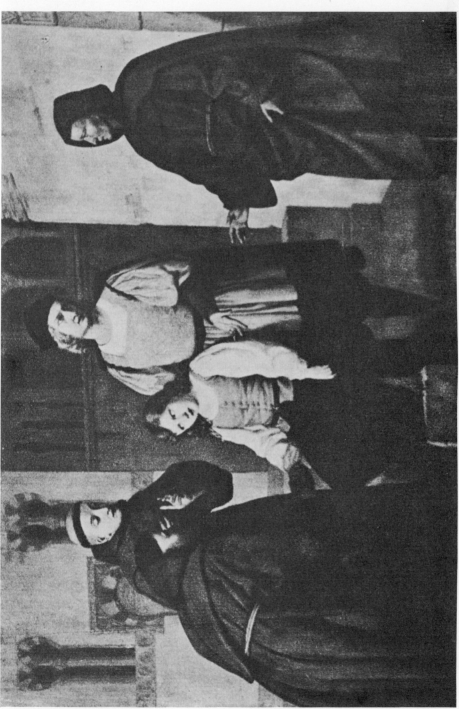

Columbus and his son Diego at the convent of Santa Maria de la Rabida. (Painting of Guistiniano degli Avancini. Galleria Nazionale. Trento.)

Santa Maria *of Julio F. Guillén (1929), named caravel.*

Nao Santa Maria. — Model by R. C. Anderson (1930), at the Addison Gallery of American Art, Phillips Academy, Andover, Massachusetts.

Catalan ship of about 1450. Model from San Simon hermitage, in Mataró (Spain), now at the Maritiem Museum Prins Hendrik, Rotterdam.

Partial view of the catalan model of ship (1450), with details of construction and rigging.

Episode of the Saint Ursule life. Retable from Cubells (Lérida, Spain) church, by Juan Reixach, 1468, in Art Museum of Catalonia, Barcelona. The shrouds of the main mast have no ratlines, but we see a man climbing ratlines, and not climbing the shrouds. By this we may assume that the painter suppressed the ratlines in order to simplify the drawing. It is clear the ballast is to port.

Seal of Louis of Bourbon, 1466.

Vittore Carpaccio (1465-1525 or 26). — 'The legend of Saint Ursule' (Galleria dell'-Academia, Venezia).

Model of the Santa Maria *under Martinez-Hidalgo's plans and direction.*

Stern of the Martinez-Hidalgo model.

Martin Alonso Pinzon, captain of the caravel Pinta.

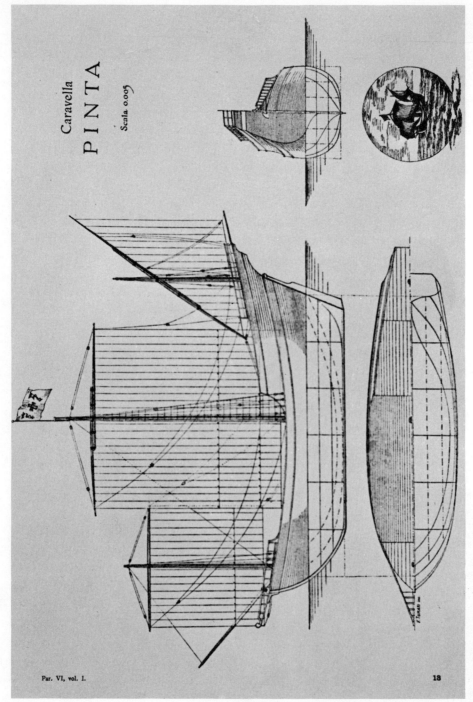

Caravella PINTA
Scala 0.005

Caravel Pinta. Plan of Enrico D'Albertis (1892-94).

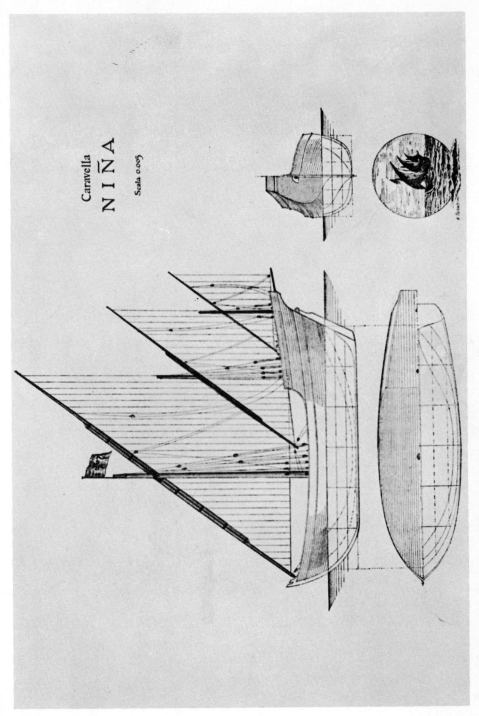

Caravella
NIÑA
Scala 0.005

Caravel Nina. Plan of Enrico D'Albertis (1892-94).

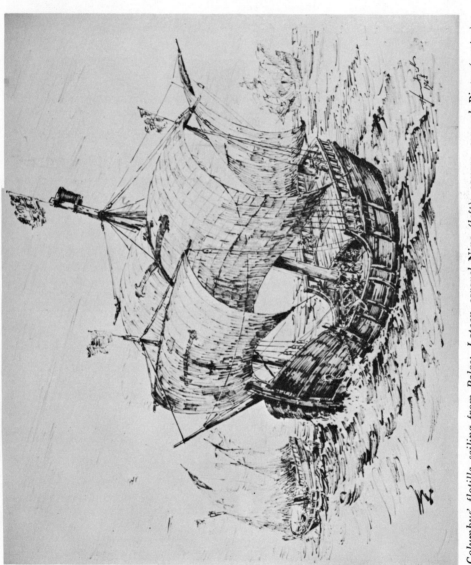

Columbus' flotilla sailing from Palos: Lateen caravel Nina (left); square caravel Pinta (centre); nao or carrack Santa Maria (right). Artistical interpretation of the reconstructions by Martinez-Hidalgo (1963)

Columbus iconography: 1. Anonymous from the end of the sixteenth century or beginning of the seventeenth cent. (Musée de Versailles). 2. Cristofano dell'Altissimo (Galleria degli Uffizi, Florencia). 3. Anonymous from the end of the sixteenth century (City Hall, Genoa). 4. Anonymous from the end of the sixteenth century (?) (Marquis Gianneto Pareto, Spinola, Genoa). 5. Saint Christopher, in the Juan de la Cosa chart. To some people this is a Columbus portrait. (Museo Naval. Madrid). 6. Anonymous from the first half of the seventeenth century. (Musée de Rouen). 7. Portrait by Antonio Rincon (Collection Rosselly de Lorgues). 8. Engraving by Henry Lefort from a portrait in Museo Naval, Madrid. 9. Anonymous from the seventeenth century (Biblioteca Nacional, Madrid).

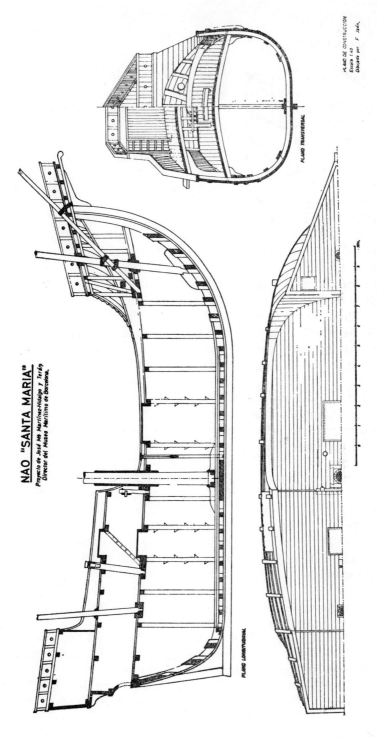

NAO "SANTA MARIA"

Proyecto de José Mª Martínez-Hidalgo y Terán
Director del Museo Marítimo de Barcelona.

PLANO DE CONSTRUCCION
Escala 1:40
Dibujado por F. Jain.

PLANO TRANSVERSAL

PLANO LONGITUDINAL

Santa Maria — Construction plan of Martinez-Hidalgo (1963).

a tun of wine. The coamings are low and the hatch is fitted with plank covers and tarpaulins. Between the mainmast and mizzen, on this deck and under the quarterdeck, is a similar hatch to the hold and to a storeroom, to avoid having to use the main hatch at sea to obtain stores, which might be dangerous to the ship in heavy weather. There is a hatch in the quarterdeck over the after main deck hatch. There is no hatchway in the bows.

Forward of amidships, on the main deck, are two bilge-pumps; the barrels are bored out of logs and the pump-rods are also of wood. The valve is of leather, shaped somewhat like an inverted umbrella. Bronze pumps came into use only a little later when Diego de Rivero invented a pump that won him an award from Carlos I. In 1531 one of Rivero's metal pumps, in a test, was found to pump ten times more water than the old wooden pumps, such as used in the *Santa Maria*.

There was an old Spanish seaman's idea that if the bilge water stank they would be happy, for it was a sign that the ship did not leak and that they would not have the labor of much pumping. If the bilge smelled too unpleasant, because of foulness in the bilge, they could flush her out and wash the hold with vinegar. This relation of pumps to foul water in the minds of seamen is illustrated by a remark of Salazar regarding two city fountains, or pumps, "whose water neither the tongue or palate would like to taste nor the nose to smell, or the eyes to see, as the water comes out foaming like hell and stinking like the devil."

Under the entrance arch to the forecastle, which Winter called "Arch of Triumph", is the bitt, a curved beam above the deck reaching from bulwark to bulwark and projecting outboard slightly at the ends. For a long time this bitt-timber was not understood; by some it was considered to be a windlass, this, in spite of the fact that it could be seen in many representations of naos of the 15th century. The timber is well shown in the Mataro model (Winter indicates the bitt on his profile plan, but does not show the crown nor the beam at all in the plan view or in section). The anchor cable was bitted on this timber, as is plainly shown in the xilograph of a nao in the *Libre del Consolate* nao of 1502. The cable passed below through scuttles in the main deck or through the hatch covers of the main hatch.

There seems to be no known reference to the use of a windlass to work the ground-tackle. Apparently only capstans or "crabs" were used and these were portable. These were used for setting up the main halyards and other heavy gear, as mentioned in *Livro Nautico,* the famous manuscript containing valuable information on the Portuguese caravels of the 16th century. The capstans used in the reconstruction of the *Santa Maria* were modeled on those used on board or ashore for working heavy gear or for careening.

Seven anchors were carried by the nao, four forward, with two lashed to the catheads and a fluke on the rail and two warping grapnels stowed forward as well. In the hold was stowed a large sheet anchor, called *fornaresa, de esperanza o de salvacion* by the seamen. The bower anchors were 10 quintals (460 kilograms) each, with hemp cables of 80 fathoms length (134 meters). The spare sheet anchor was heavier. The grapnels were 1 and 2 quintals (46 and 92 kilograms). The anchors were of the well-known wooden-stocked type still in use, but their shank was longer and arms thinner and somewhat longer in proportion than was the later form. The spades were triangular. The stock was very heavy, reinforced with rope woolding. The large iron ring was served with spun yarn.

In the restoration, the design of the anchors took into consideration the fact that, until the 17th century, the Spanish anchors were characterized by their relatively thin shanks and arms, reminiscent of the Viking anchors. It was this that produced the old Dutch saying, "As lean as a Spanish anchor."

The ring in the crown of the anchor, for the fish pendant used to buoy the anchor or to raise it when foul, was known in Columbus' time, as shown by contemporary graphic evidence, but no trace of it is to be found in the two anchors that have been found on the north shore of Haiti, near the village of Lemonade de Bord de Mer, in the vicinity of the site of the fort of Navidad, which are commonly assigned to the *Santa Maria.* It was on the coral reefs at the entrance to Caracol Bay — very dangerous as they were just a few feet below the surface — that the *Santa Maria* was wrecked. One of these anchors, found in 1781, is now exhibited in the National Museum of Haiti, at Port au Prince, and the other was recently found by Edwin Link, working from his vessel, the *Sea Diver.* It is possible, of course, that in Columbus' time anchors were made with or without the ring, as in Viking anchors.

Salazar gives an imaginative description of a ship of the 16th century that might well be applied to the *Santa Maria*. This famous captain, whose letters have been so useful to us, said, "Some call the ship a wooden horse, others a timber coach, while still others call her a dirty bird. I call her a town or city, but not the city in Heaven described by St. Augustine, because I cannot see in her a sacred church, nor a house of justice, nor the inhabitants celebrating mass, nor even acting as if they were controlled by reason."

He went on to describe the similarities of a ship to a grim and dark city, full of bad odors, filth and uncomfortable living conditions. The lack of light in the between-decks of the ships, the stench of bilgewater, the lack of space, the numbers of rats and cockroaches, lice and other vermin, he compared to some unpleasant and poor city. His picture of shipboard life is an unpleasant one, but his description shows that life in the poorer quarters of the cities was almost equally unpleasant in his time. These conditions produced high mortality ashore and at sea in Columbus' time.

The underwater parts of the hull were protected from the shipworm (*teredo*) by a coating of tar and tallow. The creosote in the tar was the important factor in this coating. The bottom was painted by beaching the ship and then heeled by tackles and capstan (careening) until one side of the bottom could be painted. Then the vessel was floated and turned, and then heeled the opposite way. The vessel was searched, caulked and the seams payed, then the whole bottom painted with tar and then tallow. The topsides were treated with whale or fish oil, or a combination of both, which was made at Niebla (Huelva).

The reconstruction of the *Santa Maria* was designed without excessive decoration of any kind. The transom stern about the rudder port was white, as in Reixach's nao, and inside of the bulwarks and stanchions of the main deck, quarterdeck and Poop, and the forecastle, green arches with white points, as in the picture in the *Libre del Consulat,* 1502 edition. Some red paint was employed on the wales and vertical guards.

XV. *RIGGING*

The rig of the *Santa Maria* is well established — sprit-sail, fore course, main topsail, main course with two bonnets, and a lateen mizzen. Columbus wrote in his *Journal,* Wednesday, October 24,

1492, "Then came a very good breeze and I set all the sails of the ship, main course with two bonnets, the fore course, sprit-sail, mizzen and topsail."

The most powerful sail, the one that produced the most drive, was the main course. The sprit-sail fore sail and mizzen, smaller than the main, served more to balance the rig and to help steering, particularly in tacking or in holding a steady course. The topsail was of little value due to its small size. In later times the main topsail was made larger in proportion to the course and by the 17th century it became an important sail in producing speed.

The fore and main courses had the canvas sail cloth sewn with vertical seams, strengthened by small square patches, as shown by Benincasa and in the Turkish carrack of "La Peregrinacion de Grünenberg." (The Pigrimage of Grunenberg.)

On the head of the sail, grommets were provided for the lacing or ropebands. The tack-cringles were eyes formed in the bolt-rope and the head-cringles likewise; the latter secured to their respective yardarms by straps passed so that cleats and seizings were omitted. To clew the courses' leach lines, clew-garnets and buntlines were used. These furled the sail. Bowlines were used, having two or three bridles, to help set the sail in going to windward by making the luff stand taut. The bowlines were led to the bowsprit, which originally existed only as a boomkin for the bowlines and for handling a grapnel and chain used to grapple an enemy's ship in boarding when in action. Bowlines were used in Viking times, as early as the 8th century.

The mainsail had no reef-points; though the Hanseatic cogs had employed them as early as the 15th century, the Southern Europeans had not, as shown by the use of the bonnets mentioned by Columbus. The sail was reduced in area, when necessary, by unlacing the bonnets in turn from the foot of the sail. The fore-course had neither bonnets nor reef-points.

The upper bonnet carried, at its top, lacings which were loops passed through the grommets in the foot of the course and through each other, to form a chain-lacing. Every tenth loop and grommet was marked by the letters *AMGP,* standing for *Ave Maria Gratia Plena;* the sailors said this *Ave,* they claimed, to "marry" the loops duly, that is, to haul them out properly. Two large loops at the center of the foot of the course secured the chain-loops when passed by a reef-knot. The lacing of the lower bonnet passed

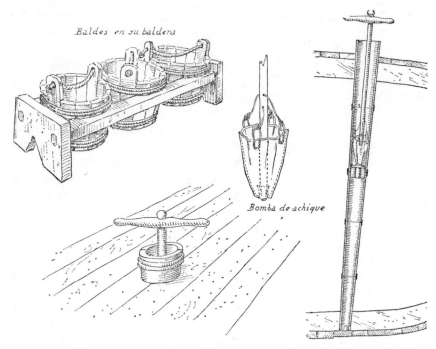

Baldes en su baldera

Bomba de achique

Pump and buckets.

through grommets in the foot of the upper bonnet in the same manner.

The sprit-sail was called the "feed-bag" by the sailors because of its fancied similarity to the feeding bags used for horses and mules in Spain. This sail apparently came into use in Spain about 1480. It was spread by a sprit-sail yard, rigged to an iron traveller— an iron ring and hook that rode on the bowsprit. When the sail was furled on its yard, both were removed and placed alongside the bowsprit, resting fore-and-aft and lashed.

The topsail, which Fernandez Duro and Guillen took from Diego Rivero's chart, made 40 years after the discovery of America and which D'Albertis also followed, was accepted as being trapezoidal in shape and sheeted to the main yardarms. But in the new reconstruction, Carpaccio, the Venetian artist, and a drawing on a Portuguese chart of very early in the 16th century, have been followed — the sail made rectangular and sheeted to the round-top. The topmast is a mere flag pole, with a small sail set on a light yard. It is believed that in Columbus' time the topmast was wholly unsupported by shrouds or runners, or by stays. Later, when the topmast was so supported, a larger trapezoidal sail was certainly used but, in the *Santa Maria*, the topmast could bear only a very small light-weather topsail.

The mizzen sail, as in all lateens, was bent to a two-piece yard, the upper part the *pena* and the lower the *car*. The yard crossed the mast at about a 40° angle and was rigged in the usual manner employing parrels, halyard, etc.

The early Egyptian vessels had sails dyed purple or striped, as had also the early Grecian vessels. Cleopatra is said, by Plutarch, to have given sails a feminine touch by painting flowers on red-colored sails. On later Roman ships the sails were sometimes decorated with paintings of a she-wolf nursing Romulus and Remus. Viking ships had striped sails, with the predominant color red. In the Middle Ages, decorative painted shields were used following Viking customs. On the Hanseatic cogs, blue crosses were sewn on both sides of the sails. During the 15th century, it was common practice to paint the sails with figures of saints and with other religious symbols. In the 17th century all kinds of decorations on sails had pretty well disappeared, to be revived in a modest way in the 19th century, in the sailing packet ships of America (and in a few British packets) with insignia of the packet lines — Black Ball, Black X, Blue Ball and Red Star — so decorated. In Columbus' time the most popular sail decoration in Spanish and Portuguese vessels was the cross. Even somewhat later this fashion existed, as shown by Pigafetta, in his description of the first voyage around the world: "Today we gave the ships new sails on which the cross of Saint Giacomo of Gallicia was painted, with the words *Esta es la figura de nuestra buena ventura* (This is the image of our good luck). Since this referred to Spanish ships, it was decided to place the red cross of Santiago on the topsail and the fore and main courses of the *Santa Maria*. This is appropriate in a nao that had been named *La Gallega*.

The rigging and spars were to be typical of the Spanish naos of the 15th century, as far as could be established. The large, heavy mainmast was still affected by the old single-masted nao rig in which speed and handling had depended upon one mast. The diameter was therefore made 65 cm. at the partners, 40 cm. at the hounds. The mast was stepped almost vertically and, together with the topmast (26.6 meters heel to truck), is longer than the hull. The mainmast is in one piece, with rope wooldings to prevent checking. When adequate timber was not available, the mast was spliced by means of fishes. The mast wedges reach to half the height between main and quarter decks, and are about the same length below the main deck. This gave the wedges the appearance of being a chimney and is the reason for the terms *fogonadura* (Catalonian), *fogonatura* (Italian), and *tcheminaye* (Provençal) being applied to the structure.

The topmast is very light and short, as in Carpaccio's nao, and those in other contemporary graphic material, with sheets led to the top.

The mainmast is supported by six heavy shrouds on each side, each set up with heart-shaped deadeyes (having the usual three eyes in each) and lanyards, on chainplates, following the representation of naos on the altar of St. Nicholas at Burgos and the carrack by "WA". Two others had the shrouds set up to the waterways. No shroud or backstay was employed for the topmast head as no representations of these had been found. The topmast is so light and weak that such rigging would not be useful anyway, particularly with the very small light-weather topsail.

Ratlines were placed on the shrouds, for access to yards and top, though Morison believed that ratlines were not in use so early. This seems questionable since ratlines appear in representations of ships earlier than *Santa Maria*. The earliest representation is on the seal of the city of Dansig.

On the foremast, ratlines were not used. The small size of this mast required only simple rigging so it was rigged with a rope ladder abaft the mast. This was the fashion in the early Mediterranean naos on their mainmasts, until they copied northern ships.

The mizzen mast was supported by runners, or tackles, typical of the lateen rig. Shrouds were not used with this rig at even much later date, except for some Dutch and other non-Mediterranean vessels in which the lateen spanker was no more than a steering sail and not trimmed on the wind. No ratlines were employed in this rig, as men rarely went aloft. The short mast could be climbed as could the lateen yard, just as in Arab vessels.

The mainmast was also supported by a heavy stay, running from the roundtop or shoulder of the mast to the stem, set up there with deadeyes and lanyards. It was not considered correct to employ a main topmast stay.

The foremast raked forward and, in height, was a little over half of the mainmast. It was therefore much lighter than the main, and was 20 to 35 centimeters in diameter.

The bowsprit was a simple pole, without a bobstay (shown in the Fernandez Duro and Monleon drawings) stepped alongside the foremast and secured there and to the stem with lashings. A light foremast stay was carried to the fore-end of the bowsprit where it passed through a block and led inboard. The mainsail bowline lead blocks and the halyard block of the spritsail were secured a little inboard of the stay block.

The mizzen mast raked aft slightly, is stepped, like the foremast, on the main deck. The height is slightly less than the foremast. In order to obtain balance of the sail plan, the tack of the lateen is forward of the poop and the sail is sheeted to the taffrail. Later this mast was placed farther aft and sheeted to a boomkin as can be seen in the pictures of Spanish and Portuguese naos on the chart of Juan de la Cosa.

The fore and main yards, and the mizzen lateen yard, were in two pieces, southern style, rather than in one piece as in the north of Europe. The doublings of these yards were long, about one-half the length of each yard. The doublings were formed with one part of the yard hollowed and the other part rounded so that they married together, on their joining faces, the whole length of the doubling, for lashing. The topsail and spritsail yards, being small and light, were in one piece. The yards were formed with short arms and shoulders, the taper of the yards or pieces being very moderate.

The mainyard is hoisted by a double tie, or halyard double-ended, which reeves through sheaves in the masthead and sets up with a double-tackle, belaying at a heavy fife-rail on the quarterdeck. In addition, lifts are employed, reeving through blocks at arms and outer thirds of the yard, employing three blocks on each side of the yard. Due to the weight of the yard, it was lowered in port and rested on the rails. No foot-ropes were used, the sail was furled after the yard was lowered. (On Reixach's representation of a nao, a sailor is shown on all fours, on top of the yard aloft, due to lack of foot-ropes. These were introduced about 1600.) The

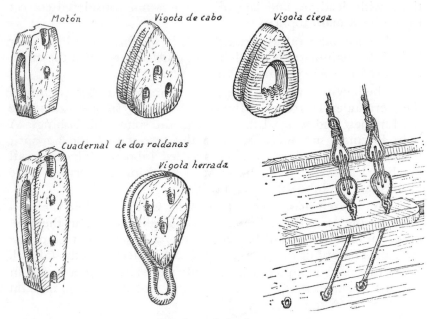

Blocks and deadeyes.

yard is attached to the mast by a parrel made up of parrel trucks, spreaders and parrel lines, following the "WA" carrack.

All running rigging was of hemp. The braces of the main and fore courses are double, those of the fore course lead to the bulwarks in the waist, near the break of the quarterdeck. In Anderson's model they lead to the mainstay, a practice apparently employed not earlier than 1520. The sheets are single parts, fore and main; it was not until about 1520 that they became double. The fore yard is rigged similarly to the main, but with single tie or halyard, small parrel and guntackle purchase lifts to yardarms only.

The bowlines' crowfoots are attached to the leech boltropes of the main course, the tricing lines lead through blocks on two series and reeve through blocks in the lower masthead in the manner shown in "WA" carrack and in the nao of *La Peregrinacion de Breydenbach.*

All standing rigging is tarred; the Spanish fibre (*esparte*) was used only for light gear that did not require much strength and also for anchor cables in fresh water where hemp rotted quickly.

The blocks were of wood, single sheave blocks are of the type shown in the Mataro model and in the "WA" carrack. Double blocks of two different size sheaves are shown in a galley drawn by Carpaccio.

The channels of the mainmast — the only place they were used — are very heavy and carry chainplates and deadeyes, as in the nao on the altar at Burgos, even though this is of 1505, for the same arrangement is shown in the "WA" carrack of 1475.

The round-top on the mainmast is built with strong frames, lined with leather and fitted with two davits by which arms — throwing-darts, or javelins, arrows, stones and other weapons — were sent aloft for fighting. The tops were the last resort in resistance, but in a merchant ship the chief use of the top was as a lookout and in handling gear.

XVI. *THE LAUNCH AND YAWL*

The nao carried two boats, a launch and a yawl. The first was the larger, having a length nearly equal to the distance between raised forecastle and quarterdeck. It was of such capacity that it would take about fifty boatloads to fill the hold of the nao. The launch was employed in loading and unloading a nao, or to take in ballast or for any heavy duty, such as laying out anchors. The dimensions used for the launch are 7.9 meters length overall, 2.9 meters beam and 1 meter depth.

The yawl was the boat used for general purposes — carrying messages, ship's officers, etc., and was about one-third smaller than the launch. When at sea this boat, like the launch, was carried on deck. To bring it aboard was a sign of departure and to clear the ship of visitors or — as the Spanish say — *Batel dentro, amigos fuera* (Boat in, friends out).

Columbus, in his journal, makes several references to the boats, as on October 14, 1492, he said, "I ordered that the nao's yawl and the caravels' launches be prepared. . . "

XVII. *NAVIGATION INSTRUMENTS*

Of the nautical instruments employed by Columbus, the first to be described should be the mariner's compass — called the "magnetic needle" in Spanish. The compass was mounted inside a small cabinet, the "binnacle," which Eugenio Salazar described as "a box similar to that used to cover the chamber-pot in a bed-room."

The mariner's compass had a circular card on which was painted the compass rose with a magnet underneath. On the center of the rose was a small cone in which the top of a brass or copper pivot pin rested, the heel of which was stepped in the bottom of a wooden bowl so that the card could turn with the least friction. The magnet was of iron and had to be remagnetized frequently; the lodestone for this purpose was carried by the pilots and was treated as a jewel of great price.

Careful observation of the compass led Columbus to discover that the magnetic variation or declination changes from place to place, from N.E. to N.W. when crossing the 3° 30' meridian, to the East of Corvo in the Azores. This was noted during his first voyage on the 13th of September. Columbus wrote in his journal on that Thursday, a day to be remembered in the history of navigation, "During this day and night sailing on the rhumb line, West, we sailed 33 leagues and counted 3 or 4 less, the currents being contrary. *On this day, in the evening, the compass needle pointed somewhat N.E. and by morning, N.W."* Columbus' route has been studied by many authorities and it is agreed that the Admiral had noticed the change in magnetic declination when he really was still to the eastward of the line of zero declination. The motion of the polar star around the pole caused the compass to show gradual change.

Although the discovery of the change in magnetic declination was made by Columbus, the existence of magnetic declination was known earlier, though Columbus' son Ferdinand, Las Casas and Herrera claimed to the contrary and attempted to credit this to Columbus also. Though magnetic declination was not a matter of general knowledge in the 15th century, the fact that the compass needle did not point exactly to the north or geographic pole had been known earlier; Humbolt (in *Cosmos*) observed: "In the 12th century of our era the Chinese not only knew of the compass, made by hanging a magnetic needle on a cotton thread which pointed at an angle to the geographic meridian, but they also knew how to measure the declination so indicated." According to Saussure, the Westerners learned about magnetic declination in the 8th century but the first records are of much later date. Hugh Lange pointed out in 1934 that the English poet Chaucer,

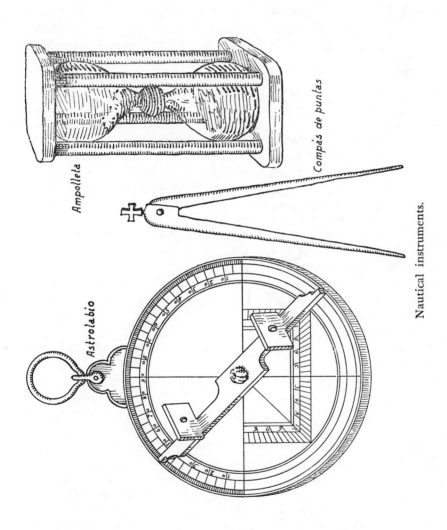

Ampolleta

Compás de puntas

Astrolabio

Nautical instruments.

author of *The Treatise on the Astrolabie,* mentioned declination in 1380. But it has been demonstrated that the quotation from the manuscript by Pedro de Advigerio in the Leyden Library is apocryphal. However, the Atlas of Andrea Bianco, made in 1436, contains some figures that presumably are related to magnetic declination. This also can be seen in a solar quadrant of 1451, in the Innsbruck Museum, as well as in a chart drawn at Nuremberg the same year as Columbus' first voyage.

Columbus did not know how to use the astrolabe on his first voyage, though he is known to have carried one. In his rare astronomical observations he used a quadrant with arms on one side to align with a celestial body, and a plumb-bob, suspended from the vertex showing the height or angle on a calibrated sector. The use of this instrument required two men, an observer and an aide who read the angle at the time of observation. The reading was usually quite inexact due to the effect of the ship's roll on the plumb-bob. Hence, the cross-staff (ballestilla), though apparently unknown to Columbus, was in more general use.

The troublesome errors in observations of the heights of celestial bodies obtained by use of the astrolabe, quadrant or cross-staff persisted for a long time after Columbus' era, as shown by Salazar's description of his voyage from the Canary Islands to Hispaniola: "Oh, how God shows his omnipotence by having placed this subtle and very important art of navigating a ship on the stupid judgment and in the rough hands of these pilots! You hear them asking one another, 'How many degrees have you logged, Your Honor?' One says, '16,' another 'nearly 20' and another '13½.' Then they ask one another, 'What is Your Honor's observed position in respect to land?' One says 'about 150 leagues' while another says 'I found 93 leagues this morning.' Whether they claim 3 or 300, none agree and none know the truth."

Among the other instruments listed as being used by Columbus are the "log-glasses," or sand-glasses, and the deep-sea leads used for taking soundings. These were also mentioned in the *Hechos de los Apostoles* (Creed of the Apostles in the Bible) with regard to St. Paul's shipwreck and were well-known in the 15th century.

The speed of the ship through the water was judged by sight and by guess; it was not until the 16th century that the rudimentary log-chip came into use. The first reference to this seems to be in Pigafetta's account of the voyages of Magellan and Elcano: "As shown by the measurement we made with the *stern measure-line,* we ran 60 to 70 leagues per day."

XVIII.   *ARMAMENT*

In several entries in his journal, Columbus mentions the bombards and refers to their stone shot. On October 7, 1492, he wrote, " . . . the caravel *Pinta* fired a bombard on sighting land and hoisted a flag to the masthead." In his entry of January 2, 1492 he wrote " . . . ordered a bombard to be made ready and to fire close to the nao, he saw how far the stone shot missed her by the fall of the shot into the sea."

The 15th century Catalonian-Aragonese naos carried from one to four bombards and, in the early 16th century, the naos fitted to go to Italy and the Barbary Coast apparently had four. This is the number that has been assigned to the *Santa Maria* and the guns are placed on the quarterdeck, as in the woodcarving of 1496 in *Estoriador de Emperador Vespaciano,* two to a side and without port lids. Gunports and lids are commonly consided to have been the invention of a French builder, Descharges, of Brest in 1501 — too late to have been used in the *Santa Maria.* One of the very early pieces of graphic evidence showing artillery between deck is, as a fact, French and of the first decade of the 16th century. It represents the *Louise,* flagship of the French fleet of the Mediterranean, and is supposed to be a copy of an earlier engraving.

The barrel or tube of the bombards was made by rolling a sheet of wrought iron and the tube was then reinforced by shrinking iron rings around it. The gun was carried on a mount formed of a balk of timber secured outboard, the inner end raised or lowered by forcing a block or chock under it. These guns were loaded at the breech, having a chamber or charger to serve as a cartridge. When ready to fire, the chamber was placed in a kind of stirrup fixed to the tube and secured by a wedge driven between stirrup and the breech of the charger. The charge was made up of gunpowder; a mixture of sulphur, saltpeter and charcoal of some variance in proportions and power. The gun was fired by a hot iron rod being brought to the touchhole of the charger. The maximum range of the stone shot used was not over 900 feet and, due to the "windage" or loose fit of the shot, accuracy could not be obtained for half that distance. The guns were pointed by maneuvering the ship, the mounts have no angle of train. In the reconstruction, the length of the tube is 1.50 meters and the bore diameter, 9 centimeters. The gun carriages or mounts were fitted with ringbolts for the breechings.

Another piece of armament in general use in the time of the *Santa Maria,* and therefore utilized in the reconstruction, was the falconet or swivel, a light gun having a breech-loading system like that of the bombards and a bore of about 5 centimeters. These were mounted on crutches or oarlock-like brackets fitted on the rails and in the top. They fired iron or lead shot, but could be used to fire small pieces of iron to serve as grapeshot or the more modern shrapnel.

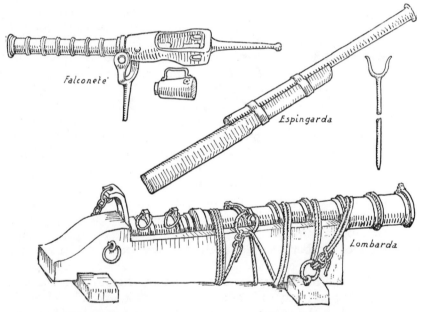

Gun (lombard), falconet and 'espingarela' (musket).

Columbus also mentions crossbows and Turkish bows throwing bolts (darts) and arrows, and swords and lances. He also had *espingardas,* a small firearm, on his first voyage. This was a hand gun formed of a bell-mouthed tube of iron or bronze secured to a heavy, wooden stock. They were muzzle-loading. The powder for these guns was carried loose in flasks and the balls in bags. The gun was usually held with the left hand and fired by a slowmatch held in the other hand. This weapon was the forerunner of the blunderbuss and pistol.

Defensive gear consisted of breastplates, helmets, and round and oblong shields painted with heraldic devices and slogans.

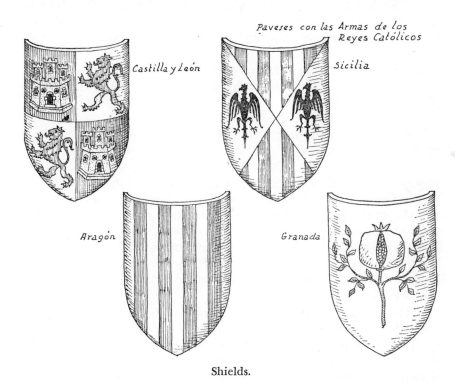

Shields.

It was normal, in Columbus' time, for ships on voyages of exploration to be well-equipped with weapons and ammunition as it was expected that fighting with the natives, in any land found, would occur.

XIX. *FLAGS AND LANTERNS*

The *Santa Maria* hoisted the flag of Castile and Leon, quartered white and red, with yellow castles over the red and red lions crowned in yellow over the white. This same flag was shown at the top of the mainmast as represented in the Castilian naos of Juan de la Cosa's chart. The mizzen-mast carried the insignia given the fleet as a special, distinctive white with a green cross in its center and on each side an F and a Y crowned the initials of Fernando and Isabel (the Y was used instead of the I in the old spelling).

The Admiral's personal flag was a standard of royal red damask with painted images of Christ crucified on one side, and one of the Holy Virgin on the other, mounted on a lance with gold cords and tassels; this standard was kept in the Admiral's cabin only to be taken from there on solemn occasions. It was carried on the starboard side on landing and in the ceremonies of taking possession of lands.

In the reconstruction of the *Santa Maria,* for dressing the ship, it has been planned to hoist red and white pennants on the mizzen-mast, and on the top with smaller triangular ones of green and white on the yardarms. To starboard on the quarterdeck, the blue ensign, with horizontal golden anchors of the Captain General of the Ocean Sea and, forward, as a jack (torrotito) a flag showing the arms of Columbus when ennobled were carried. These flags were not carried by Columbus in his first voyage, of course, but they illustrate the splendor of the honors that were bestowed on the discoverer. On the gunwales of the poop deck, shields with the coat of arms of Castile, Leon, Aragon, Sicily and Grenada are hung.

On the poop-deck there was a lantern; the mark of command carried at the stern, which was carefully watched by accompanying ships; and because of carelessness in this, more than a few incidents occurred when squadrons were on voyages. This lantern had a symbolic value similar to that given later to the flag and for many years they were the most sought-after trophy in naval battles. There have been lanterns of extraordinary artistic beauty, and in the oldest of which we have information, the wax candle was protected and shielded by panes of talc (mica), later by glass. Columbus does not neglect to say in his journal that every night he lit the poop lantern on the *Santa Maria* and after this the only light allowed was the binnacle's, to illuminate the compass. Only on exceptional instances, as during the first trip of Charles I (Carlos I), from Spain to Flanders in 1517 with an armada of 52 vessels, were other lights on board the ships. Thus, the chronicler of the Emperor says that the ladies were allowed iron lanterns

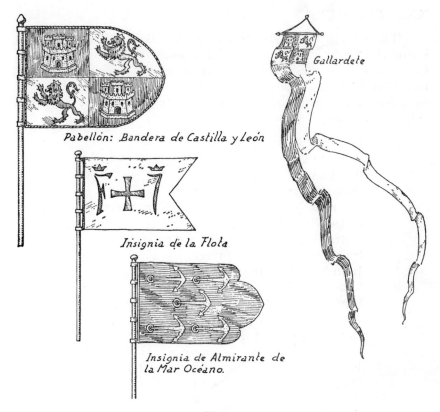

Pabellón: Bandera de Castilla y León

Insignia de la Flota

Insignia de Almirante de
la Mar Océano.

Gallardete

Flags.

when going below, but after that the Captain made an inspection and only the poop lantern, one light in the King's cabin, another in the princess Doña Leonor's cabin, one in the binnacle and one under the quarter-deck, "where the sailors take refuge when the boatswain's whistle is not calling them," were permitted. Despite all the precautions taken, Fray Prudencio de Sandoval in his *Historia del Emperador* relates that during the trip the horse-transport ship caught fire and 160 persons died from burns, among them, the second head-groom and twenty-two of the king's pages.

On board the reconstruction of the *Santa Maria,* besides the poop lantern there are several lanterns — in the cabin, in the binnacle and under the poop and forecastle decks.

XX. *THE CREW*

The American investigator, Miss Alice Bache Gould, to whom is due the credit for the most reliable study of the composition of Columbus' crews, has given the names of eighty-seven of the ninety men that made up these crews. On the *Santa Maria,* it is believed that, from captain to boys there were forty, and the list comprises thirty-nine names, as follows:

Cristobal Colon, admiral
Juan de la Cosa, master and owner
Peralonso Niño, pilot
Diego de Arana, master-at-arms
Rodrigo de Escobedo, admiral's secretary
Pedro Gutierrez, steward
Pedro Sanchez de Segovia, paymaster
Luis de Torres, interpreter
Juan Sanchez, surgeon
Chachu, boatswain
Domigo de Lequeitio, boatswain's mate
Antonio de Cuellar, carpenter (?)
Domingo Vizcaino, able seaman and cooper
Lope, caulker
Juan de Medina, able seaman and tailor
Diego Perez, able seaman and painter
Bartolome Bibes or Vives, able seaman
Alonso Clavijo, able seaman
Gonzalo Franco, able seaman
Juan Martinez de Açoque, able seaman
Juan de Moguer, able seaman
Juan de la Plaça, able seaman
Juan Ruiz de la Peña, able seaman
Bartolome Torres, able seaman
Juan de Xeres, able seaman
Rodrigo de Xeres, able seaman
Pedro Yzquierdo de Lepe, able seaman
Cristobal Caro, silversmith and apprentice seaman
Diego Bermúdez, apprentice seaman
Alonso Chocero, apprentice seaman
Rodrigo Gallego, apprentice seaman
Diego Leal, apprentice seaman

Pedro de Lepe, apprentice seaman
Jacomo el Rico, apprentice seaman
Martin de Urtubia, apprentice seaman
Andres de Yebenes, apprentice seaman
Juan, apprentice seaman
Pedro de Terreros, steward's mate
Pedro de Salcedo, ship's boy

The master, or captain, had the total command of the ship but, in the case of the *Santa Maria,* he actually was the second in command because of the presence of an admiral on board. The pilot was in charge of the ship's navigation and everything connected with it, and at times was the only expert on board, but not on the *Santa Maria*. However, on the outgoing trip, Peralonso Niño was closer than Columbus to the truth in the dead reckoning of the distance sailed. The pilot had to take along charts, astrolabe, compass, quadrant, sand-glasses and sounding-leads and also had knowledge of the tides. Alonso de Chaves said that "the pilot in a nao is like the mind in a human body."

The boatswain, the master's deputy, carried out the master's and the pilot's orders, distributed the work of the crew, supervised the stowage, inspected the rigging and gear, supervised the general cleaning and freeing of the bilge, the airing of the sails and seeing that the fire in the fireplace (fogon) was out at sunset. The Admiral's secretary prepared reports and the acts of possession of lands discovered and he kept records of everything that was loaded or unloaded, and also of the consignees, and acted as a notary public in drawing wills. The mission of the master-at-arms of the fleet was to discipline offenders. The paymaster kept a book of the expenses and was custodian of the share of any treasure that belonged to the Crown. The steward was in charge of the water, wine and victuals, and also of the candles, fuel for the fireplace, teaching the apprentices to box the compass, and the prayers said when turning the watch-glasses. He had to make sure that the men were awake when on duty. In distributing the rations, he had to be certain that the older food was used first, keeping always on his person the key to the storeroom. The carpenters, outside of their regular professional work and maintaining tools, nails and spare wood, had to care for the bilge pumps. The caulker was in charge of maintenance of water-tightness of the vessel for which purpose he had special tools and supplies — oakum, oil, tallow, pitch, scupper-nails, lead sheets and everything necessary for stopping a leak. The cooper cared for the tuns, casks and barrels, caulking and replacing staves, and the silversmith assayed the minerals and gold found.

A nao's crew worked for a monthly wage, or for a share. In the latter case, the total value of the freight was divided into three shares and the captain had two — one for the nao and another to cover the provisions and expenses incurred by him during the trip. The third share of the freight was distributed among the crew in the following manner: to the master, four shares (soldadas); to the pilot, same as the captain; to the boatswain, two shares; the secretary, steward, carpenter and caulker, the same as the boatswain; each sailor, one share; to the gunners, one soldada and two-thirds; the apprentices, two-thirds of a soldada; and the boys, only one-third.

The crews of Columbus' vessels drew a fixed wage, however, the captains and pilots, 2,000 maravedises a month; the sailors, 1,000; and the gromets, (apprentices) 666. The monthly payroll for the three ships amounted to 250,180 maravedises, and the total expenditure for fitting the flotilla out was, in round figures, two million maravedises, comparable (according to Morison) to $14,000 today.

XXI. *LODGINGS AND FOOD*

The *Santa Maria* had a raised quarter-deck, over the main-deck, which formed the stern-castle crowned by the poop-deck. It is to this stern-castle that the *Journal* refers when on Thursday, October 14th, it states, ". . . because the Admiral, at ten o'clock at night and being in the stern-castle (under the poop-deck), saw a light."

On the 18th of October, relating to the visit made by an Indian chieftain of Puerto Rico, Father Las Casas transcribes verbatim this description by Columbus, giving an idea of his cabin on board the flagship: "He (the little king of Hispaniola) entered the nao and he found that I was eating at the table under the stern-castle. He quickly sat down next to me and did not give me an opportunity to eat. I thought that he would like to eat our food and ordered something for him. When he first entered under the stern-castle he had signaled with his hand to his people to remain outside, and this they did promptly and respectfully. They all sat on deck, excepting two old men who, I thought, were his counselors or officers. They came and sat at his feet and, of the food that I placed before them, he took from each a sample and sent the rest to his people, and all partook of it, and did the same thing with the drinks; he just touched them with his lips and then gave them to the others, all graciously and with few words. The words said, so far as I could understand, were pleasant and the two men looked and talked to him with much respect. After they ate, one of their servants had a belt that looked like the Castilian belts in shape only, of a different workmanship, this he took and gave to me, and two pieces of engraved gold that were very thin, so that I believe that little is obtained here. I understand, however, they are very close to the place where it is obtained and where there is a great deal. I saw that he liked some finery that I had over my bed and I gave it to him, and some amber beads as well that I had around my neck, also some red shoes and a vial of orange flower water, that made him marvelously happy. He and his officers and counselors were very sorry not to understand us and I could not understand them. Nevertheless, I could understand that he said that if I needed something from here, the whole island was at my orders. I sent for some trinkets, among which was a token, an ancient gold coin on which Your Highnesses are sculptured. I showed this to him and I told them as I did yesterday, that Your Highness had mastered all the most powerful in the world, and that I had never seen a greater prince. I showed them the Royal flags and the others with the cross, and told them how great lords Your Highnesses are to send me from so far away without fear, and many other things that he believed marvelous."

This cabin must have been small and it is probable that originally it did not exist, the quarterdeck being flush to the taffrail, as in the nao *Libre del Consolat* (1502), or the nao on the chart of Juan de la Cosa. Perhaps it had then a mere tent resembling the one shown in the nao of the altar of Juan de Reixach, or on many others of the same period.

But when she was chartered for the expedition, it is very probable that the quarterdeck was fitted structurally to lodge the Admiral with dignity and to maintain the privacy that at all times has been considered convenient for the commander. The *Journal's* description leads to such a supposition.

COLUMBUS' SHIPS

In this cabin, reserved for the exclusive use of the Admiral, there was not much room for furniture. The furniture, therefore, has been reduced to a table, chair, stool, coffer, trunk, desk, tableware, washing stand and bed, with a bed cover and drapery like that which Columbus presented to the Indian chieftain in Hispaniola.

The interior may have been decorated with some simple Gothic motives — shields, armor, sword, lamp, an interpretation (copy) of Toscanelli's chart, astrolabe, quadrant, compass, a Royal standard, flags of Castile and Leon, flotilla's flags and some other objects, not forgetting the rosary and an image of the Virgin Mary in the advocation of Our Lady of Guadalupe, to which Columbus was devoted, as shown in his *Journal*. It was the practice to offer her vows, when they were safe after one of the storms faced on the return trip.

The officers slept on mattresses or in simple bunks under the quarterdeck out of the way of the tiller. During the day the mats were rolled up, placed in sacks of Spanish grass and stowed on the bulwarks or in the hold. But it is probable that the captain, the pilot, or both, had "centinas" in the hold. (*Centina* was a narrow cabin, also called *celda*, cell). It is also possible that in good weather the boatswain slept in the storeroom with some of the other minor officers.

The mats had also another use, to serve as shrouds, in the case of death. Gonzalo Fernandez de Oviedo, who despite his rank had slept on such a poor bed, mentions this fact in the chapter *Misfortunes and Wrecks* in his *Historia General de Indias*: "A sailor trying to get his hands on a Spanish grass mat that was under the mattress on which I was laid, was told by the servant: "Don't take that mat, you can see that the captain is dying, and when he is really dead, there will not be another to wrap him in to throw to the sea." This I heard perfectly and sitting up on my bed and very angry, I said: "Take the mat, I will not die at sea nor will God wish me to lack sepulchre in the land!"

The sailors slept in any corner of the upper deck and Fernandez Duro assures us that it was forbidden for them to sleep in the hold, the purpose being to have them at hand for any emergency. It is not probable, however, that on the *Santa Maria*, with such a large crew, this military discipline would be required. The solution to the problem of the sailor's bed was eventually found in the hammocks of the American Indians.

Personal belongings were carried in chests or coffers, whose number and sizes were limited in relation to rank. Thus, by an agreement signed in 1050 for the trip of Vicente Yañez Pinzón, it was settled that the captain and pilots were allowed to carry a chest not bigger than five palms (a measure of length from the thumb to the end of the little finger extended) in length by three in height; the sailors' one chest between two, the apprentices one between three, and the boys one between four.

For their meals they had troughs (gamellas), wooden plates, earthenware soup plates and knives and drinking-horns for the water ration.

The provisions loaded included water, wine, oil, lard, flour, biscuits or hardtack, bacon, salt, vinegar, chick peas, kidney beans, lentils, onions, snap-beans, garlic, olives, dried and salted fish, rice, sugar, quince meat, honey, cheese, almonds, raisins, figs, and other dried fruits in an amount sufficient for a year. The basic foods were the biscuits, bacon, chick peas, salted meats and cheese. Ferdinand Columbus said that he had seen many eating their "mazamorra" — spoiled broken biscuits — at night time when the worms that thrived in the dampness of the hold could not be seen.

It is probable that they had only one hot meal a day, about eleven o'clock in the morning before the change of the watch, the weather permitting. It surely was not an easy task to cook in the firebox, on a tripod or on an iron plate, with only the bulwarks for protection against the wind, with enough sand for insulation for the fire, while the ship rolled violently taking water over the rail. The dirt or sand under a fire had another meaning after some lookout had cried "land" only to learn later that it was only a low cloud he had sighted. The next time he hailed, some doubting-Thomas would reply, "Yes, the dirt (land) in the fire-box."

The captain, the master, the pilot and the secretary ate at the table and the dinner was announced by an apprentice with these words: *"Table, table, sir captain and master and good company, table ready, food is ready, water as usual for sir captain and master and good company. Long live the King of Castile by land and sea! Who says to him war, off with his head; who won't say amen, get nothing to drink. Table is set, who don't come won't*

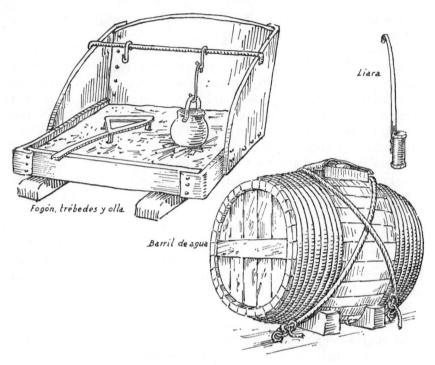

Liara

Fogón, trébedes y olla

Barril de agua

Cooking-stove, water cask and water measure.

eat." The sailors, without excepting any such resounding calls, went to the vicinity of the fire-box, "the island of the earthern pot (olla)," they call it, when their sense of smell led them to hope that the *ollaos were already boiled* (ollaos=eyelets). They extended their soup plates and told the boy, "Put on the mizzen!" and looked for a seat on the coils of rope or on the coamings of the hatchway or in the most protected place available.

Salazar describes the dining of the crews with his typical exaggerations, but it is the best description of this subject ever made: "In the twinkling of an eye the sailormen sit to their table on the floor, keeping the seat of honour for the coxswain. One throws his legs backwards; the next, his feet in front; another kneels down; still another rests on his side; and others in all kinds of positions and, without saying grace, these knights of the round-table pull out their knives of different shapes made to kill hogs or to skin lambs or for cutting bags, and then grab in their hands the poor bones and peel them clean of their sinews and meat, as if all of their lives they had practiced anatomy in Guadalupe or Valencia. In a prayer, they leave them as clean as ivory. On Fridays, or on Fast days, they eat their snap-beans boiled with water and salt. On important holidays they eat codfish. A boy moves around with the beverages in hand and with his cup he gives each of them a little of some very bad wine, more suited for church ceremony than for drinking. Eating thus, the first course last and the last first, with a middle course between, they complete their dinners without satisfying their hunger. Ask for a drink in the middle of the ocean, you will die from thirst because they will give you water only in ounces, as from a drug store, and this after filling up on bacon and salted meat, for Madam Sea does not care to preserve meat or fish unless they are coated with her salt. And, in spite of this, most of the things to eat are rotten and stink with a smell like some savages' stews. And even with the drinking water you have to forget your senses of taste and sight in order to swallow it. Thus you eat and drink in this likable condition. And if, in drinking and eating, you get this kind of a deal, what could it be like in other things? Young and old, dirty and clean, they are all stuck with each other, and thus one burps, another breaks wind, some relieve their bowels, you dine and you can't tell them they are uncouth, for the laws of this association allow anything."

And the toilet function? Just over the gunwale until the day arrived in which they installed a seat of ease; this was considered an unusual refinement and, using a delicate euphemism, it was named *the garden.* Later on, Salazar wrote, that in order to accomplish the function they had to hang themselves over the sea and make reverence to the sun, and to its twelve signs, hanging to the rigging, that had to be washed every day. And in order to relieve the crudity of the description, he wrote in the Galician language.

XXII. *VESTUARY*

The clothes of the sailors consisted of a loose blouse with a hood, stockings, and a red wool cap (this cap was similar to the Catalonian "barretina," as one can see in the Zephyrs representing the mild breeze in the painting on the chart of Juan de la Cosa).

Naval seamen did not wear a uniform in Spain until the 19th century, but the officers were uniformed in the 18th century. Only when there were persons of royal blood aboard or of the upper class, clothes of red color, in use since the time of Alphonse X the Wise, were issued to the sailors. The only distinctive mark of the seamen in those times was the red bonnet, and in the time of Columbus the red bonnets from Toledo were famous; there is no doubt that they had several on board the *Santa Maria*. In the diary there is mention that the Admiral gave several to the Indians and used one of these bonnets to draw lots with chick-peas and rosemary, in accomplishing the vows made during the storm of Feb. 14, 1493. (By the way, the first one to draw the lot was Columbus himself.)

The style of the stockings (leotards) and the loose blouse with a hood used in Columbus' time can be seen on the altar piece of St. Nicholas in Burgos (beginning of the 16th century). Another garment that was very common was the overcoat of brown cloth; they used to call it "papahigo," the "main sail," since it was also the biggest and warmest garment of seamen and because of the use that Columbus made of it. Some authors supposed that the Admiral was wearing the Franciscan habit, when it was really this kind of anguarina (overcoat) of Old Castille. In the same manner, there is proof that Columbus used to dress in red color, so traditional among sea people (the red and the blue colors became the mark of the Spanish navy when the uniform was introduced), as one can see from the diary, when he says that he took off a gala cloak with a hood in order to give it to the Indian chief Guacanagari, to whom the Admiral also gave, some days before, red shoes.

XXIII. *LIFE ON BOARD*

During the day the sailors, when not busy with the rigging, washed the decks, spun oakum, mended the sails, pumped the bilge and did other chores. They were divided into two watches or gangs, one watch being on duty at a time.

The dawn of day was announced by the singing of a boy of the duty watch:

> *Blessed be the light of day*
> *and the Holy Cross, we say;*
> *and the Lord of Veritie*
> *and the Holy Trinity.*

Blessed be th' immortal soul
and the Lord who keeps it whole,
blessed be the light of day
and He who sends the night away.

After the *Pater Noster* and the *Avemaria* (Hail Mary), he added:

"*Dios nos de buenos dias; buen viaje; vuen pasaje haga la nao, señor capitan y maestre y buena compana, amen; asi faza buen viaje, faza; muy buenos dias de Dios a vuestras mercedes, senores de popa y proa.*"

"*God give us good days, a good voyage, a good passage to the ship, sir captain and master and good company, so let there be, let there be a good voyage; many good days may God grant your graces, gentlemen of the afterguard and gentlemen forward.*"

In turning the seventh sand-glass of the dawn's watch, that is half an hour before the seven A.M. relief; the deck washing done, an apprentice seaman sang:

"*Buena es la que va,*
mejor es la que viene;
siete es pasada y en ocho muele,
mas moliera si Dios quisiera,
cuenta y pasa, que buen viaje faza."
"*Good is that which passeth,*
better that which cometh,
seven is passed and eight floweth,
more shall flow if God willeth,
count and pass makes voyage fast."

And when all the sand of this glass ran out it was seven o'clock, the apprentice did not repeat the chantey that had been sung on the half hour but called the men who formed the new watch, in this way:

"*Al cuarto, al cuarto, señores, marineros du buena parte, al cuarto, al cuarto en buena hora de la guardia del senor piloto, que ya es hora; leva, leva, leva.*"

"*On deck, on deck, gentlemen mariners of the starboard*

watch, on deck in good time, you of Mr. Pilot's watch, for it's duty time; shake a leg!

Before starting the first night watch the boatswain quenched the fire in the galley and, when turning the sand-glass, an apprentice said:

"Bendita sea la hora
en que Dion nació
Santa Maria que le parió,
San Juan que le bautizó.
La guardia es tomada,
la ampolleta muele,
buen viaje haremos
si Dios quiere."

"Blessed be the hour
in which God was born,
Saint Mary who bore Him
Saint John who baptized Him.
The watch is called,
the glass floweth;
we shall make a good voyage
if God Willeth."

And during the night, in a muttering of voices, at times muted by the wind and the sea, you would hear at every half hour:

"Una va pasada
y en dos muele;
mas molera
si mi Dios querra,
a mi Dios pidamos
que buen viaje hagamos;
y a la Madre de Dios y abrogada nuestra,
que nos libre de agua, de bomba y de tormenta."

One glass is gone
and now the second floweth;
more shall run down
if my God willeth.
To my God let's pray
to give us a good voyage;

and through His blessed Mother
our advocate on high,
protect us from the waterspout
and send no tempest nigh."

Then he called to the lookout forward:

"Ah, de proa, alerta, buena guardia!"

"Hey you! forward, look alive, keep good watch."

At which the lookout was supposed to shout "Good watch!" to prove that he was awake. This tradition has been kept in the Spanish Navy to this date, where in making the nightly rounds the calls are:

"Good watch, starboard lookout!"

And this, after checking his side light, answered:

"Bright green!"

And then the leading seaman of the watch will call again:

"Port lookout, good watch!"

And the answer came:

"Bright red!"

The lookout at the bow will also announce:

"Bright top!"

The daily routine on board the ships of the great discoverers was altered on Saturdays by the singing of the Salve, and Eugenio de Salazar explained it this way: "On Saturday and with the altar ready and candles burning, the *Salve* starts and everybody sings. We were all throats. We sang in unison, not by thirds, fifths and octaves, but singing all eight tones and fourths at the same time. Sailors are partial to divisions so they divided the four winds in 32 parts; in this same manner they have divided the eight musical tones into thirty-two cruel, resounding and very dissonant tones in such a way that we succeeded in transforming this day dedicated to singing the *Salve* and litanies into a hurricane of music. If God and His glorious Mother and the Saints — to whom we pray — looked at our tones and voices instead of our hearts and souls, it would not be expedient to ask for mercy with such disordered howling.

"When we are over the Salve and the litanies, said by the Captain that acted as a priest, we will pray in reverence to the blessed Apostles, asking them to pray for us and give us a good voyage.

"Afterwards all believers recite the *Credo*. Then a boy that acts as an acolyte says: "We will recite a Hail Mary (Ave Maria) for the ship and company." The other boys answer: ' Be welcome." And then we all pray the Hail Mary. After the boys stand and pray: "Amen and God give us a good night." And this ends the day's ceremonies customary on Saturdays."

XXIV. *QUALITY OF THE CREWS*

A great deal has been written about Columbus' first voyage, with reference to its planning and its tremendous consequences, in which the spirit of enterprise shown, the character and behavior of Columbus and the subsequent political, cultural and religious results, are described. But, in general, few voices have been raised in praise of those obscure men of the crews of the ships whose contributions had such an important effect upon the voyage. Few remember that the men who shipped with Columbus as seamen, apprentices, and ship's boys could not expect public recognition and their names being recorded in history. On the contrary, the impudent, false legend was soon established to prey upon them, crucifying them as criminals, convicts, ignoramuses, with other insults of similar nature.

Who were these men who by the strength of their muscles, by hardship and by discipline, made possible the successful culmination of the project developed by the more-or-less enlightened mind of the originator and leader, and of the other, resulting projects?

As to the claim that the King had pardoned men involved or accused of criminal or civil delinquency in order that they might be shipped by Columbus — which was a common practice in those and in later days in Spain and elsewhere, when great risks were involved — there was one example in Columbus' crews. This was the case of a Bartolome Torres, a citizen of the town of Palos, who was under a death sentence of hanging on the charge of having killed a man during a fight. He had been liberated under Royal pardon. It is readily appreciated that a murder committed in the heat of passion during a brawl, perhaps accompanied by other aggravations, does not necessarily indicate that the condemned man was an abandoned criminal or a perverted and wicked individual. This sole case cannot be used to base a general accusation against the crews. ¶ .o.

Miss Alice Bache Gould, in her scholarly and brilliant research, has been able to identify 87 members of the crews. Of these, four were foreigners — one Portuguese, one Genoese, one Calabrian and one Venetian. The identifications of the last two are somewhat doubtful. The possible presence of English and Irish sailors has not been firmly established. Of known Spanish nationality, there was one from Murcia, ten from northern Spain, and the balance were from Andalucia. Most of those of known family origin were of the Palenses from Palos and Gallegos from Galicia, as well. Aside from these there were the uncle and nephew of Gil Perez, father and son of Pedro Arraez, and two brothers of the Medel family. The squadron was comprised of "home-town" ships and, as the distinguished American marine historian Samuel Eliot Morison wrote, "All in all, it seems to me that Columbus' shipmates were 'good guys,' hardy, competent and loyal to their commander."

Another slanderous claim is the fiction that Columbus sailed with crews of undesirable and undisciplined character. This seems to be based upon a comment by Las Casas on a passage in the journal, when the wind veered to the S.W. on September 22, " . . . contrary winds were very desirable since the crews had become uneasy, having come to the opinion that the winds were never favorable for a return to Spain." This incident could not have been very important as no acts of insubordination are mentioned. Columbus would have been aware of griping by the crew in his small ship. Such complaining would be natural in seamen after 17 days at sea from the Canaries, particularly in men believing in superstition, such as witchcraft and traditional "horror" stories. The passage may well indicate Columbus' relief in the possibility of stopping, for a while at least, the griping.

In later years there are records of fighting and mutinies caused by prolonged suffering from lack of food and water, unseaworthy ships, and severe weather; even now people often become irritable and complain after two weeks at sea in small craft. Griping and homesickness were undoubtedly present and Columbus must have been both aware and tired of complaint, but there is no evidence in the Journal that there was a serious disciplinary problem.

The command of a ship on such a voyage as Columbus' required special personal qualities of a psychological nature and there is evidence that Columbus was lacking. He had difficulty in obtaining complete obedience, and, compared to the admiration extended him in other aspects, there is little proof that he was a good leader of men. It could be said of him, in general, that he was an unusually good observer, a good navigator for his time, a poor leader and a worse colonizer. His selfishness, and jealousy of another's glory, is shown — he even envied the honor given a humble lookout and seized the 10,000 maravedises (the so-called *eye income* [renta de ojos]) that had been promised by the King to the first man to see land. This dishonorable incident led to the invention of a fable that the lookout, Rodrigo de Triana, who should have received the reward, was so angered by Columbus' act that he rejected Christianity and became a Mohammedan. The truth is that he became a ship captain and died while in command in the South Seas, as part of the ill-fated Loaysa expedition in which Elcano, the great captain from Guetaria and the first to circumnavigate the earth, met his death.

It should be remembered that Cristobal Quintero sailed as a seaman on the *Pinta,* which he owned, a fact not mentioned by some historians who respond only to a dusty manuscript, without feeling for the human beings they write about. To anyone who appreciates the work done by the crews of Columbus' ships, without thought of return, the men themselves are worthy of respect and praise. The crews had a very important part in the great voyage and faced the unknown and immense Atlantic and its perils, known or imagined, with steadiness and fortitude.

PART III
The Nina *and The* Pinta

XXV. *REFERENCES*

THIS discussion is about two caravels, typical of the type and both from the western Andalusian coast. The *Nina*, a lateener when sailing from Palos, was a good example of the original rig of her type. *Pinta*, though previously a lateener, had been converted to square rig sometime before the voyage began, showing the transition in rig brought about by experience in Atlantic Ocean voyages.

Patriotism has caused some Portuguese authors to deny Spain any part in the development of the caravel but history is definite regarding the Andalusian contribution. The latter had found the deficiencies of the lateen rig when sailing long distances with the wind on the quarter and it occurred to them to change the rig in a manner to improve it for ocean voyaging. If the caravel was three-masted, the mainmast (which was a little forward of amidships) remained in its place or was moved aft a little. The foremast was usually shifted forward and both masts crossed yards — the Portuguese usually crossed yards in the foremast only, but they eventually followed Spanish practice and crossed yards on

COLUMBUS' SHIPS

fore and main. The crossing of yards had been applied to *Pinta* before leaving Palos and to *Nina* on her arrival at the Canaries.

If the caravel was two-masted, as may have been the case with *Nina*, a foremast was stepped (usually the original mizzen); the mainmast remained as it was, or was shifted a little aft and a new lateen rigged mizzen mast was fitted.

Carabela "NIÑA"

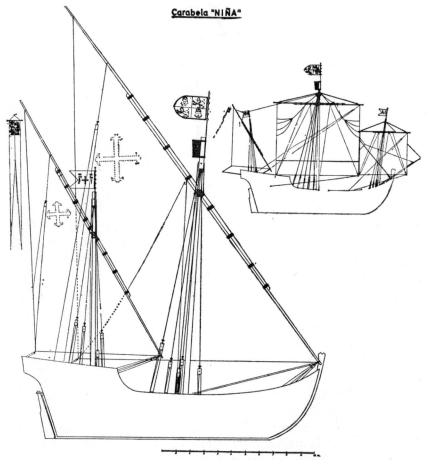

Sail plan of the *Nina* as a lateen caravel and transformation in a square caravel. Design of Martínez-Hidalgo, 1963.

Though fame surrounds *Santa Maria*, of the three vessels of Columbus' squadron, the *Nina* was the most serviceable and the best vessel of the lot. "If it were not for the caravel . . . very good and well-rigged, I would fear of being lost," Columbus wrote after a storm during the return voyage in February 1493. The Admiral always liked the *Nina* and of the seventeen ships brought together for the second voyage, he chose her as his flagship for the exploration of Cuba. He owned 50 percent of her and on her he returned to Spain in 1496 carrying 100 men, after the loss of his vessels in the hurricane of 1495. On her arrival at Cadiz she made a voyage to Italy and near Sardinia she was captured by a pirate but her crew recovered her, and she made another voyage from Cadiz to Hispaniola early in 1498, as part of Columbus' squadron in his third voyage. Columbus sailed her about 25,000 miles, and the last record of this stout little caravel is of a voyage to the Pearl Coast of Africa in 1501 (Alice Gould, *Boletin de la Real Academia de la Historia,* LXXXVII, Madrid, 1926).

Built at Moguer, on the bank of the River Tinto, she was a credit to the local shipwrights, who were competitors to the noted Portuguese shipbuilders of the Algarve region. *Santa Clara,* the original name of the *Nina,* has been practically forgotten. She was built for a trader and designed to sail with 5½ points of the wind. The *Santa Maria,* for comparison, could not fetch much better than 9. The *Nina* is the only vessel of Columbus' squadron whose tonnage is directly referred to — Michele Cuneo, who made a round-voyage to Cuba in her in 1494 states that she was of "about 60 tuns" and in the Italian voyage of 1497 it is stated that she carried 51 tuns (Recolta, II, ii, 103, line 18), nearly her maximum capacity. If the figure of 55 tuns, more or less, can be accepted as her approximate capacity, she seems to have been an average caravel of her time, in size.

The *Nina,* like the *Pinta,* had a flush main deck from bow to stern. It is not necessary to argue this point with an experienced seaman since no one of knowledge would consider it proper to sail an undecked, open vessel of such size in the ocean trades. Nevertheless, it has been repeatedly stated by uninformed writers that the caravels were open boats. In all fairness, however, it should be stated that this incredible idea can be traced to an error in translation of Eden, in 1555, of a passage in *De Orbe Novo,* 1516, where Peter Martyr stated: *"tria navigia: unum onerarium caveatum, allia duo mercatoria levia, sine cavis que ab Hispanis caravela vocantur."*

COLUMBUS' SHIPS

By translating *cavea* for *cubierta* (deck) instead of *gavia* (top-sail), or *cofa* (top), the error was established and this error was kept alive by Fernandez Duro. The *cavea* of the chronicler does not relate to *cueva* but to *gabia* (jaula) referring to the *gata* of a galley and the *gavia* of the naos, which later was called *cofa* or *top*. As D'Albertis and Alcala Galiano have made abundantly clear, the correct translation was: *"Three vessels; one of burden with round-top, the other two merchant vessels without round-top, called carabelas by the Spaniards."* Peter Martyr refers to the caravels of Columbus' second voyage in a way that settles any doubt that would exist, when he stated, *"duas aliquanto grandiores atque ad sustinem caveas, propter malorum magnitudinem aptos"* or *"two considerably larger and fit for carrying round-tops, considering the size of their masts."* This led to Morison's caustic comment: "Obviously, masts do not hold up decks!"

Much less is known about the *Pinta* as all records of the ship end with her return from Columbus' first voyage. Her sailing qualities were about those of the *Nina*. It seems she was a bit faster running with the wind on the quarter but *Nina* was the more weatherly. In tonnage there was not much difference, though tradition claims *Pinta* to have been the larger of the two. This tradition seems to be based upon two points: one, that she was commanded by the elder of the Pinzon brothers, Martin Alonzo and two, that she had a larger crew. D'Albertis raised another point — that *Nina* did not have a master on board so he concluded that she was the smaller. However, it is possible that *Nina*'s owner, Juan Nino, filled the position on *Nina*, though not so rated.

The crews of *Nina* and *Pinta*, as listed by Alice B. Gould, were as follows:

NINA

Vicente Yañez Pinzón, captain
Juan Niño, master and owner
Sancho Ruiz de Gama, pilot
Maestre Alonso, surgeon
Diego Lorenzo, steward
Bartolome Garcia, boatswain
Alonso de Morales, carpenter
Juan Arraez, able seaman
Rui Garcia, able seaman

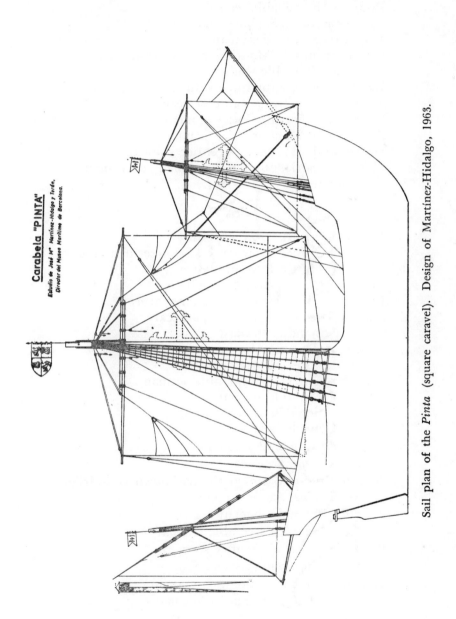

Carabela "PINTA"

Estudio de José Mª Martínez-Hidalgo y Terán,
Director del Museo Marítimo de Barcelona.

Sail plan of the *Pinta* (square caravel). Design of Martinez-Hidalgo, 1963.

Rodrigo Monge, able seaman
Bartolome Roldan, able seaman
Juan Romero, able seaman
Pedro Sanchez de Montilla, able seaman
Pedro de Villa, able seaman
Garcia Alonso, apprentice seaman
Andres de Huelva, apprentice seaman
Francisco Niño, apprentice seaman
Pedro de Soria, apprentice seaman
Fernando de Triana, apprentice seaman
Miguel de Soria, apprentice seaman and captain's
    servant.

PINTA

Martin Alonso Pinzón, captain
Cristobal Quintero, owner with able seaman's rating
Francisco Martin Pinzón, master
Cristobal Garcia Sarmiento, pilot
Juan Reynal, marshall or master-at-arms
Maestre Diego, surgeon or apothecary
Garcia Fernandez, steward
Juan Quintero de Algruta, boatswain
Anton Calabres, able seaman
Francisco Garcia Vallejo, able seaman
Alvaro Perez, able seaman
Gil or Gutierre Perez, able seaman
Diego Martin Pinzon, able seaman
Sancho de Rama, able seaman
Gomez Rascon, able seaman
Juan Rodriguez Bermejo (better known as Rodrigo
    de Triana), able seaman
Juan Veçano, able seaman
Juan Verde de Triana, able seaman
Pedro de Arcos, apprentice seaman
Juan Arias, apprentice seaman
Fernando Medel, apprentice seaman
Francisco Medel, apprentice seaman
Alonso de Palos, apprentice seaman
Juan Quadrado, apprentice seaman

Pedro Tejero, apprentice seaman
Bernal, apprentice seaman and captain's servant.

XXVI. *PREVIOUS RECONSTRUCTIONS*

In 1892 the Government of the United States placed an order for the construction of two versions of the *Nina* and the *Pinta* with the shipyard of Miguel Cardona (Barcelona). Lieutenant C. McCarty Little was assigned to the project but he found it difficult to find a yard willing to do the work, due to budgetary reasons. Finally he contracted the construction with the above-mentioned shipyard with the intention of utilizing the hulls of two coastwise sailing vessels that had made previous trips to America. The designs for the two caravels came from the board of the painter of the Naval Museum, Rafael Monleon, the collaborator with Fernandez Duro in the reconstruction of the *Santa Maria*. The results were not very satisfactory because the hulls selected were not adaptable to the peculiar lines of a caravel and, in addition, they cut off the sterns, which caused the shortening of the runs necessary for speed and steering. When they tested the vessels under sail, they found that they were ungovernable. The 30th of September the two vessels sailed from Barcelona to Huelva, towed by the American gunboat *Bennington*, to participate in the celebration of the 400th Anniversary of the Discovery of America. Later on, one of them was towed by the same gunboat and the other by the cruiser *Newark*, and arrived at Havana on the 9th of April, 1893. In that port they embarked Spanish crews under the command of Lieutenants Juan Vignau and Pedro Vazquez de Castro, sailing again on the 16th, under tow with the *Santa Maria*, commanded by Concas. After sailing up the St. Lawrence River, calling at Quebec and Montreal, they arrived at their destination, Chicago, to be exhibited at the Columbian World's Fair. After some years, one of the caravels caught fire and was destroyed; the other sank in 1918-19.

The *Nina*, as reconstructed, was rigged with three masts with the three lateen sails. Her dimensions were: length on deck, 19 m.; waterline length, 18.33 m.; keel length, 16 m.; beam, 6.33 m.; width at the wing transom beam, 4.65 m.; depth, 3.85 m. The rig then given *Pinta* cannot be accepted today because it was a very complete nao's rig like that of the *Santa Maria* — with sprit-sail, fore stay-sail, mainsail, topsail, and lateen mizzen — and to give the appearance of a nao, Pinta was given a forecastle. Her dimensions were: length on deck, 24.0 m.; length on waterline, 20.0 m.; keel length, 18.65 m.; beam, 8.33 m.; wing transom beam, 4.65 m.; depth amidships, 4.43 m.; depth aft 9.33 m.; depth fore, 6.33 m.

Monleon made other studies of Columbus' vessels, namely that of the *Santa Maria* with a square stern and the rig proportions of a half a century later. In his study of the *Pinta* he fell into the mistake of considering her a lateener, as was the *Nina* at the start of the first voyage. In placing the shrouds of the mainmast he used channels, dead-eyes and lanyards, all of which were improper for the lateen rig. He was also mistaken in placing the step of the mizzen-mast on the poop-deck, without providing the necessary strength, and also in that the main mizzen yard could not be swung without hitting the deck in changing tacks. He called the *Santa Maria* a caravel on the pretense that there was no difference in rig between a caravel and a nao, and in stating that the only difference was the prestige given by her use as a flagship; it has been shown earlier how mistaken was this criterion.

D'Albertis was right when, in his study of Columbus' vessels, he showed the difference between the hull of a nao and that of a caravel, making the latter sharper-ended, even though he followed Escalante in some later conclusions. In order to establish the principal dimensions of *Pinta* he started with a supposed depth of hold capable of three layers of pipes. In Escalante's opinion, these required 4.5 cubits, equivalent to 2.52 m., plus another half cubit (0.28 m.) for the floor timbers, and still another cubit (0.56 m.) for loss of stowage space. He obtained a depth of hold of 6 cubits (3.36 m.). The ratio of depth of hold he made 1 = 2.16 m. and, 7.28 m. The ratio of beam to length would be 1 = 3.46. m., making the length equal to 45 cubits = 25.20 m. Though his conclusion is logical, in view of the fact that the caravel was "long and narrow," the traditional formula of 1 to 3 would be modified in this case, reaching 3.46, exceeding somewhat his own specifications.

In the case of *Nina*, D'Albertis maintained that the depth of hold and the beam were equal, cutting down the length two cubits, which seems to be proper because the ratio then remains of 1 to 3.3 and therefore the resulting measurements were: depth of hold, 6 cubits = 3.36 m.; beam, 13 cubits = 7.28 m.; length 43 cubits = 24.08 m.

In the matter of rig he made *Pinta* a square-rigger and *Nina* a lateener, as she was at the start of Columbus' first voyage. The ratios of the sail plans are acceptable, but not the stepping of all masts vertically (en candela) without the rake that follows the flaring of the stem and stern, as D'Albertis should have observed in so many vessels of the same class in his own country.

At a later date D'Albertis received from the City Government of Genoa the commission to make the models shown today at the Museum Civico Navale at Pegli, Italy. It is surprising to see in these models that the *Pinta* has been given a round-top and top-sail, breaking away from the design that he prepared earlier, more in accord with the "sine caveis" mentioned by Peter Martyr. Also, it is improbable that the sprit-sail can be added to the model; he did right in reinforcing the hulls with the knee-riders not shown in the drawings. If you leave aside the vertical masts, the rig of his model of *Nina* is superior to that of Monleon in the calculation of the sail plan (centers of effort) and in the general tackle arrangements that make a rig practical.

In 1962, Carlos Etayo, a Lieutenant in the Spanish Navy, had built in Pasajes (Guipuzcoa), the so-called *Nina II*. Under his command she was towed from Guetaria to the latitude of Vigo and from there she sailed to Palos, where she arrived after an uneventful voyage. The historical confluence of the rivers Tinto and Odiel, on one of whose banks is located the Monastery of La Rabida, was to be the starting point of a new voyage, retracing the route of Columbus. After calling at Las Palmas, under sail, he tried to reach Gomera, Columbus' port of call, but the lack of favorable winds forced him to desist and he then continued with the Atlantic crossing, arriving at San Salvador after seventy-six days and many hardships. The vessel sailed and handled very poorly.

Shortly before his trip, Etayo published a book "*La Santa Maria, la Pinta y la Nina* and, based mainly on the drawings on the first chart of Hispaniola, shown at the Biblioteca Columbina at Seville which we have already described, he deduced the probable measurements that in his opinion would be used in Columbus' vessels. Shortly before his departure from Spain Etayo came to Barcelona to discuss his book with me, a copy of which he had just sent to me. As I told him then, we could only agree in that the *Santa Maria* was a nao; *Pinta*, a square-rigger caravel, and *Nina*, a lateen caravel. In dimensions, rigging and general aspects our points of view greatly differed. In his version, Etayo gave *Nina* the following dimensions: maximum length, 13 m.; beam, 3.36 m.; depth of hold, 1.96 m., with the resulting tonnage about one-half of that of the original *Nina*. Moreover, it is known that the caravel carried about one hundred passengers on her return trip in 1496, an impossible feat for a ship the size of Etayo's, to whom I gave my opinions frankly and showed to him the plans and models that are published here. I have great admiration for the courage and stamina shown by Etayo, and his crew, in the hard and long crossing of the Atlantic, carried out under very severe weather conditions, but I believe much of the difficulties he suffered were due to the improper design and size of *Nina II;* the hull-form being wholly unsuited for speed and handling under sail.

XXVII. *NEW VERSIONS OF* "NINA" *AND* "PINTA"

The system followed in the new reconstruction of the two Columbus caravels, as in the case of the nao, differs radically from those used by other authorities and we believe it rests on a sounder basis.

As in the case of the *Santa Maria,* we first tried to establish the capacity of the hold and thereafter we tried to keep inside of the ratios known to have been used in the Spanish caravels and their Portuguese sister ships.

Nina

Thanks to Cuneo, the precious information about the tonnage of her hold is available — around 60 tuns or a little less. And because we consider that the *Livro Nautico* (Portuguese) continues to be the best source concerning caravels, we utilized from it the different ratios between the principal dimensions of the "carabela antigua" — the "old caravel" — that are given there. These ratios are: beam to depth of hold = 2:30 m.; keel to beam = 2.40 m.; length to beam = 3.33 m.

Using these ratios we designed a hull whose calculated tonnage was somewhat under 60 tuns. Of the several experimental designs, the closest to these ratios was selected, and from this we constructed a half-model, as had been done with the nao. For the general hull-form we had in view the best models of xebecs (jabeques), exposed in the Museo Maritimo de Barcelona, as the caravels belonged to this family of Mediterranean vessels for they certainly had some characteristics in common. Both were sharp, narrow, flush-decked, good sailers with much the same gracefulness and basic design. Thus we arrived at the final model, in which we can see the caravel that is shown in the Spanish and Portuguese documents of the years around 1492. It also was considered that the modern Arabian *baggala* has the stern and sometimes a mid-section very similar to that of the caravels; also, the stern of a contemporary Arabian *sambuck* is reminiscent of that of the lateen caravels. As a consequence, we have given the *Nina* the following dimensions: length overall, 21.44 m.; length on deck, 20.10 m.; keel, 15.46 m.; beam, 6.44 m.; depth of hold, 2.80 m.; draft, 1,78 m.; tonnage, 52.72 tuns.

Her general lines agree with the design of the lateen rigged, two-masted caravel, represented in Juan de la Cosa's chart. The stern is square, as in the caravels drawn in the chart and shown more clearly in the Kuntsman chart of the coast of Brazil. This type of square stern was formed by planking tranversally or diagonally (to the vertical centerline) down to the water line or a little below, as accepted by most of today's archeologists as correct in the caravels. This is logical because it allows sharper lines in the lower part of the hull, a characteristic also agreed upon in the caravels, distinguished as they were by their turn of speed and easy working. Neither could be far from the builder's mind as an easy method because one only had to have experience in the building of a round tuck stern of the nao to learn the difficulties produced by pronounced curvature in the buttocks on the round tuck near the transom.

The reconstruction of the *Nina* is intended to show her as she was when she sailed from Palos. She was then lateen rigged; the sail plan will indicate how she could have been changed into a square-rigger at the Canaries.

The deck beam curvature is 0.63 m. and the deck sheer 0.75 m. In the waist there is a hatch of 7½ hands (1.57 m.) to allow passage of tuns of 1 m. x 1.50 m., and another under the quarter-deck allowing entrance to the storeroom when at sea without opening the main hatch, a practical arrangement for loading and unloading operations. The space between the frames is 0.60 m. and the height of the waist is 1.0 m. The midsection is 0.50 m. forward of the half length of the keelson. Other information can be obtained from the construction drawings.

The quarter-deck rigging has a height of 1.65 m. at the waist. This deck is clear, with only the fittings that are essential to the rigging.

A dismountable capstan, similar to those in use quite recently on Mediterranean feluccas or lateeners, was probably used in handling ground tackle and for other tasks that required much power. These also could be landed for careening operations when caulking the bottom became necessary.

There is always someone who argues that the lateen caravel, that sailed from Palos, was *Pinta* and not *Nina*. This mistake was introduced by Las Casas' erroneous transcription of a passage in the *Journal* — Thursday, August 9th, where: *"Hicieron la Pinta redonda porquera latina." "They made Pinta into a square-rigger as she was a lateener."* But other historians of that time attributed the transformation to *Nina*, as was done by Ferdinand Columbus who says, "to enable her to follow the other ships easier and with less danger." The modern specialist has no doubts about this point and even Cesare de Lollis corrected the text on his second edition of the *Journal*.

The reason for the change was the known behavior of the lateen rig when sailing with the wind on the quarter or before the wind; the yawing is continuous and the helmsmen are soon exhausted by having to move the tiller continuously from side to side, often without the required results. Also, the danger that sails might come aback and even jibe; if the wind changed suddenly it could require the heavy work of shifting the lateen yards, while the square-riggers, like *Santa Maria* and *Pinta*, sail perfectly with only bracing the yards required as the wind shifts.

The transformation of lateen vessels into square-riggers, following the Spanish patterns, was also made by the Portuguese in the XVI century, as soon as they appreciated its advantages. The most generalized procedure in changing a lateen caravel into a square-rigger was to step a foremast well forward; if the vessel was a three-master, the mainmast was moved somewhat aft and the mizzen remained just as before; if a two-master, as we believe was the case with *Nina*, the mizzen mast was shifted forward and became the foremast, the mainmast was moved aft a little and a new mizzenmast was stepped to balance the rig. On the foremast a square sail (called "redonda") was fitted and above this another of the same form but smaller (top-sail or gavia) was added which in due time became the fore-top-sail. This was an improvement but not impressive — a "mongrel" rig, as Fonseca called it, and with a lack of aesthetic equilibrium that is shown in the modern barkentines of three or four masts. However, this was the sail plan of the square-rigged Portuguese caravels in the XVI and XVII centuries.

The practical use of the square-rig in the caravels, and the possibility that topsails were not used, is shown in these passages in Columbus' journal; Thursday, February 14th, 1493, while scudding before a fresh gale, he wrote: "She carried her course very low, as only to skip the waves. . . ", " . . she carried only the course, low . . . ", "and sailed in this way only with the forecourse . . . the square main course had been lowered." On February 15th, was added: ". . . put bonnet on the mainsail," and on March 4th when preparing for a new storm: ". . . had to lower the course because there was nothing else to do."

We consider that the re-rigging at Las Palmas was done by shifting the mizzen forward to become a foremast and that fore and main topsails were omitted. On the foremast and mainmast, square courses were certainly fitted, the mainsail with bonnets and in the mizzen, naturally, a lateen. Also, it is probable that they installed a bowsprit for working the bowlines of the mainsail, to get better results from the rig when hauling on the wind.

The final result of the change was a rig like that of *Pinta*, without the topsails and sprit-sail that would have complicated things because of the need of a higher mainmast or of a topmast, round-top and the corresponding gear.

PINTA

Pinta has been considered a square-rigged caravel from her departure from Palos, though originally she had been a lateener, as the caravels were in her time. Otherwise, Columbus would have mentioned her lateen rig and her transformation into a square-rigger, as he did with *Nina*. The dimensions may have been somewhat larger, as has been said. Also Herrera and other historians mention her as second: "Fitted out a flagship that he named *Santa Maria;* the second, *Pinta,* and the third, *Nina,* carried lateen sails . . . ." It can be noticed that, once more, only *Nina*'s lateen rig was mentioned.

Following methods similar to those used in the reconstruction of *Santa Maria* and *Nina,* dimensions were established for the *Pinta*: total length, 22.55 m.; length on deck, 21.05 m.; keel, 16.15 m.; beam, 6.75 m.; depth of hold, 2.92 m.; draught, 1.85 m.; height of upper deck, 1.65 m.; height of gangway, 1.50.; tonnage, 60.91 tuns. As *Pinta* left Palos as a square-rig, her bow has been raised, with a small raised forecastle deck that makes her more seaworthy and allows a better stepping for the bowsprit. The rig is reduced to a square foresail, a square mainsail (with bonnets) and a lateen mizzen without sprit-sail or top-sail or a round-top but a basket (crow's nest) facing aft of the mainmast, as in the galleys. The mainmast, like the foremast, follows the old Mediterranean style, runners to the waterways instead of shrouds and because of this no channels are required, revealing in this fashion the fact that she was originally lateen caravel in rig.

The scantlings are comparatively smaller than the nao's and reflect the characteristic lightness of construction of the caravels.

Appendices

APPENDIX I

THE JOURNAL'S REFERENCES TO THE SANTA MARIA AS A NAO

... came to the *nao* a pelican ... (Wednesday, September 19th)
Two pelicans came to the *nao* ... (Thursday, September 20th)
... many flying fishes flew into the *nao* ... (Friday, October 5th)
They saw robbins and a green reed close to the *nao*. (Thursday, October 11th)
... they came to the *nao* on rafts ... (Saturday, October 13th)
At the break of day I ordered the preparation of the *nao*'s boat and the boats
    of the caravels ...
... and after I returned to the *nao* ... (Sunday, October 14th)
... I left for the *nao* ...
And I was at the *nao*'s stern ...
... which arrived at the *nao* ...
... and had his raft placed on the *nao* ... (Monday, October 15th)
... on board the *nao* ...
... I sent the *nao*'s boat ...
... this that come here on the *nao* (Tuesday and Wednesday, October 16th
    and 17th)
... I returned to the *nao* ... (Wednesday, October 17th)
... I sent the caravel "Pinta" to the E. and S.E. and the caravel "Nina" to the
    S.S.E., while I with the *nao* went to the S. E. .... (Friday, October 19th)
... I was with the *nao* anchored in this island ... (Saturday, October 20th)
... bring to the *nao* ten quintals ... (Sunday, October 21st)
... we carried all the sails of the *nao*: mainsail with two bonnets and the

forecourse, sprit-sail and mizzen, and a top-sail . . . (Wednesday, October 24th)

. . . The Admiral decided to return to the *nao* . . . (Sunday, November 4th)

. . . At daybreak he ordered to lie by the *nao* . . . (Monday, November 5th)

. . . because the *nao* was beached . . .

Today I had the *nao* lying to . . . (Tuesday, November 6th)

. . . yesterday came alongside the *nao* a raft with 6 young men, and five entered the *nao* . . . (Monday, October 12th)

Returning to the *nao* . . . (Friday, November 16th)

. . . sent the boats of the *nao* and the caravels.

After the *nao* was anchored . . . (Tuesday, November 27)

. . . does not allow the *nao* to work on the fastenings . . . (Saturday, December 8th)

. . . they brought the woman, very young and beautiful, to the *nao* . . .

. . . sent some persons with her to the *nao* . . .

. . . they told the Admiral that they did not want to leave the *nao* . . . (Wednesday, December 12th)

He had him and his canoe brought on board the *nao* . . .

. . . and took him on the *nao* . . .

. . . they came to the *nao* . . .

. . . the king came to the *nao* . . . (Sunday, December 16th)

. . . he had the *nao* and the caravel dress ship . . .

. . . some of the *nao* . . .

. . . arrived to the *nao* . . .

. . . the way he entered the *nao* . . .

. . . came to the *nao* after the king . . . (Tuesday, December 18th)

The *nao* may stay . . . (Thursday, December 20th)

. . . with the oldest rope in the *nao* . . .

. . . they came to the *nao* . . .

. . . the Indians he brought in the *nao* . . .

. . . full canoes came after them to the *nao* . .

. . and there was the *nao* . . . (Friday, December 21st)

. . . they came alongside with their canoe . . . Saturday, December 22nd)

. . . they returned with a gentleman, to the *nao* . . .

. . . to the *nao* over one thousand persons . . .

. . . and before they arrived to the *nao* . . .

. . . more than five hundred came swimming to the *nao* . . . (Sunday, December 23rd)

. . . that yesterday came to the *nao* . . . (Monday, December 24th)

. . . the sailor that steered the *nao* . . .

. . . and the currents drifted the *nao* . . .

After, the master of the *nao* . . .

The caravel did not want to receive them . . . and because of this they returned to the *nao* . . .

. . . the *nao* already had the seas break over her . . . (Tuesday, December 25th, Christmas Day)

. . . he ordered to cut down the top-mast and lighten the *nao* . . .

COLUMBUS' SHIPS

... the space between frames opened but not the *nao* . . .
The Admiral went to the caravel to place, in safety, the *nao*'s crew on the
caravel . . .
... and afterwards went to the *nao* . . .
... to unload everything of the *nao* . . .
... in the *nao* as in the watch . . . (Tuesday, December 25th, Christmas Day)
... load and unload the *nao* . . .
... sorrow that he had for loosing the *nao* . . .
... ground there the *nao* . . .
... and the *nao*'s boat . . .
... when the *nao* ran aground . . .
... that the *nao* grounded there . . .
... drop the anchor astern to pull off the *nao* . . .
... the *nao* could be saved . . .
... because they said that the *nao* was too heavy and not adapted for discovery work . . .
And carry such a *nao* . . .
... everything on board the *nao* . . . (Wednesday, December 26th)
... alongside the *nao* that was grounded . . .
... as it passed the *nao*'s side . . .
... with everything carried by the *nao* . . .
... and the *nao*'s boat . . . (Wednesday, January 2nd)
... and Our Lord ordered that *nao* to remain there . . . (Sunday, January 6th)

APPENDIX II

THE JOURNALS REFERENCES TO PINTA AND NINA AS CARAVELS

It unshipped the rudder of the *caravel* "Pinta" . . .
... of whom was the *caravel* . . .
... for not being able to help said *caravel* . . . (Monday, August 6th)
... leave the *caravel* "Pinta" . . . (Wednesday, August 8th)
... to rig the *caravel* "Pinta" . . . (Thursday, August 9th)
... they from the *caravel* "Nina" . . . (Friday, September 14th)
... Captian of the other *caravel* "Pinta" . . .
... three days passed on the *caravel* . . . (Tuesday, September 25th)
(Guillen mistakenly says that Columbus names the *Santa Maria* "caravel,"
when he really makes reference to "Pinta." [*La Parla Marinera en el Diario
del Primer Viaje de Colon,* page 48]. It will be enough to read carefully
another paragraph of the same day's run: "Today, Martin Alonso, with
"Pinta," a very good sailer, did not wait, because he had hailed the Admiral
from his caravel to say that he had seen a large number of birds going
West . . . " Though Guillen insists on his interpretation, not seeing the
mistake made in the transcription, which should read, "hailed the Admiral,"
instead of "the Admiral hailed.")
... two pelicans one of which was stoned by a young man of the *caravel* . . .
(Thursday, October 4th)
... the *caravel* "Nina" that was ahead, being a swift sailer . . .

... of which they thought the *caravel* "Nina" . . . (Sunday, October 7th)

... the ones of the *caravel* "Pinta" . . .

The ones from the *caravel* "Nina" . . .

And because the *caravel* "Nina" was a better sailer . . . (Thursday, October 11th)

At day's break I ordered to prepare the yawl boat of the *nao* and the launches from the *caravels* . . . (Sunday, October 14th)

... on board the *caravel* "Nina" . . .

... the *caravel* "Nina" . . .

... did not want to enter the *caravel* . . .

... the other raft towed astern by the *caravel* "Nina" . . . (Monday, October 15th)

... and Martin Alonso Pinzon, captain of the *caravel* "Pinta" . . . (Wednesday, October 17th)

... at dawn I weighed anchor and sent the *caravel* "Pinta" to the E. and S.E., and the *caravel* "Nina" to the S.S.E. and with the *nao* went to the S.E. (Friday, October 19th)

... The *caravels* anchored . . . (Saturday, October 20th)

... I anchored and also the *caravels* . . . (Sunday, October 21st)

The Indians that sailed on the *caravel* "Pinta" . . . (Tuesday, October 30th)

... he ordered them to go on the *caravel* "Nina" . . . (Saturday, November 17th)

... with the *caravel* "Pinta" . . .

... that he ordered placed on that *caravel* . . . (Wednesday, November 21st)

There he fetched a lateen yard and a mast for the mizzen of the *caravel* "Nina . . . (Sunday, November 25th)

... he sent the ship's boats of the *nao* and the *caravel* (Tuesday, November 27th)

... he ordered the *caravel* "Nina" to go ahead . . . because she was a swift sailer . . . and before the Admiral arrived where the *caravel* was plying to windward . . .

The *caravel* as he did not see light . . .

... the *caravel* approached . . . (Wednesday, December 5th)

... he had the *nao* and the *caravel* dressed up. (Tuesday, December 18th)

... escape to the *caravel* . . .

The *caravel* did not want to receive them . . . and for this reason they returned to the *nao;* but first went to her the *caravel's* boat. The Admiral went to the *caravel* to see about the safety of the *nao's* crew in the *caravel* . . . (Tuesday, December 25th, Christmas Day)

... to the *caravel* "Nina" . . . the king at on the *caravel* . . . (Wednesday, December 26th)

... the king of that land came to the *caravel* . . .

... as the *caravel* "Pinta" . . . (Jueves, December 27th)

... came to the *caravel* the king's nephew . . . (Saturday, December 29th)

... left the *caravel* "Pinta" . . .

The Admiral returned to the *caravel* . . . (Sunday, December 30th)

... parted from the *caravel* "Pinta" . . . (Monday, December 31st)

COLUMBUS' SHIPS

... if he had with him the *caravel* "Pinta" ...
And if it was true that the *caravel* "Pinta" ... (Thursday, January 3rd)
... he saw the *caravel* "Pinta" coming ...
Martin Alonso came to the *caravel* "Nina" ....
... the *caravel* recovered much gold ... (Sunday, January 6th)
... he had the *caravel* cleaned and caulked ... (Monday, January 7th)
... he ordered the *caravel* furnished with water and firewood ...
... those that he placed on the *caravels* as captains ...
... returning to the *caravel* ... (Tuesday, January 8th)
... went to the *caravel* "Pinta" ... (Tuesday, January 10th)
... to speak with the Admiral on the *caravel* ...
... pointing to the *caravel* astern ...
... they returned soon to the *caravel* ... (Sunday, January 13th)
... he came to the *caravel* ...
... they jumped into the boat and came to the *caravel* ...
... the *caravels* leaked badly near their keels ...
... the large amount of water taken by the *caravels* ... (Monday, January 14th)
... four young men to the *caravel* ... (Tuesday, January 15th)
... Both *caravels* leaked badly ...
... Because of the danger of the *caravels* leaking ... (Wednesday, January 16th)
Here came a pelican to the *caravel* ... (Thursday, January 17th)
... moved around the *caravel* ... (Friday, January 18th)
... arrived on the *caravel* "Pinta" ... (Monday, January 21st)
Waiting often for the *caravel* "Pinta" because she was poor to windward ...
(Wednesday, January 23rd)
In the Admiral's *caravel* ... (Sunday, February 10th)
... the *caravel* "Pinta" started running ... (Thursday, February 14th)
... from the *caravel* to the shore ... (Friday, February 15th)
... where they would place the *caravel* ... (Monday, Feburay 18th)
... three men from the *caravel* remained there ...
... and came to the *caravel* to arrest the Admiral ...
... enters the *caravel* ...
Seeing that they did not get to the *caravel* ...
... that he go to port with the *caravel* ...
... those staying in the *caravel* ...
... not to descend nor leave the *caravel* (Tuesday, February 19th)
... they climbed to the *caravel* ... (Friday, February 22nd)
Came to the *caravel* a very large bird ... (Monday, February 25th)
... they raised the *caravel* ...
... to go with the *caravel* to the city of Lisbon ... (Monday, March 4th)
... with the ship's boat armed, to the *caravel* ...
... that he send the master to the *caravel* ...
... merrily he came to the *caravel* ... (Tuesday, March 5th)
A very large number of people came today to the *caravel* ... (Thursday, March 7th)

COLUMBUS' SHIPS

... the weather was not appropriate to sail with the *caravel* ...
... and his people and the *caravel* ... (Friday, March 8th)
... ready to leave Llandra for the *caravel* ...
Arrived to the *caravel* during the night ... (Tuesday, March 12th).

APPENDIX III

THE JOURNAL'S REFERENCES TO THREE COLUMBUS VESSELS AS CARAVELS

... the pilots of the three *caravels* ... (Wednesday, August 8th)
... sailed from the said island of Gomera with his three *caravels* ... (Thursday, August 9th).

Columbus' Chronology

1451
April 22: Isabel of Castilia born in Madrigal de las Altas Torres

August 22 - October 31: Christopher Columbus born in Genoa

1452
May 10: Fernando of Aragon born in Sos

1461 (approx.)
First voyage of Christopher Columbus; probably a short trip around the coast to which he referred later in the Book of the Prophecies (1501) writing: "at a very young age I began ocean voyaging and I have continued this up to the present. This same art inclines one that follows it to wish for understanding of the ills of the world."

1465
Beatriz Arana, mother of Fernando Colon, born in Santa Maria de Trasierra (Cordova)

1469
October 19: Marriage in Valladolid of Isabel de Castilia and Fernando de Aragon

1474
Trip of Columbus to Chios, probably in the ship "Roxana," of Savona. In his diary of his first trip to the New World, Columbus refers to his trip to Chios twice in the chapters covering the periods of November 12 and December 11.

1475
New trip of Columbus to Chios in the ships of Niccolo Spinola and Paolo de Negro, sailing from Genoa. At the fall of Constantinople in 1453, the Turks,

COLUMBUS' SHIPS

in exchange for a year's tribute, permitted Genoa to continue the administration of Chios.

1476

May 31: Columbus leaves Noli with a fleet of four Genoese ships and a Flemish urca, loaded with resin lentisco, bound to Lisbon, England, and Flanders. Columbus was probably on board the "Bechalla," the Flemish urca, as a sailor, since his name does not appear in the list of officers and passengers. August 13: Between Lagos and Cape San Vicente, the Genoese were attacked by the French-Portuguese fleet, commanded by the French privateersman (corsario) Guillaume de Casenove. After a hard fight, with heavy losses by both parties (3 Genoese ships were sunk and 4 of the enemy's) Columbus, who had been wounded in the battle, was shipwrecked on the Portuguese coast; finally he reached Lisbon. In the last part of this year (1476) Columbus was in Flanders, and on the coasts of Germany, Great Britain, and Galway (western coast of Ireland). His arrival in Galway is confirmed by a note from him in *Historia Rerum,* by Aneus Silvio: "The men of Cathay, that are found in the Orient, have come close to here. We have seen very curious things especially in Galway, in Ireland; a man and a woman of extraordinary appearance in two row boats which were drifting."

1477

Possible arrival of Columbus in Ireland, as he claimed in a letter to his son Fernando: "I sailed in 1477, in the month of February, beyond Tule, an island of 100 leagues, whose southern part is separated from the Equator by 73 degrees and not 63 degrees as some authors say, and it is not on the line that bounds the west, as Ptolmey says, but is more to the westward. To this island, which is as large as Britain, the Englishmen go with merchandise, especially the people from Bristol, and at the time I went there, the sea was not frozen, even though there were huge tides, so much that in some parts, (twice a day) the sea went up 26 brazas and came down also twice a day in height." Tule (Thule) is, of course, Iceland and in reference to its latitude, really of 63.5 degrees at the southern end, Columbus was very mistaken.

1478

Columbus sailed from Lisbon to Madera to load sugar for Genoa, he reached his destination but was only partly loaded, having been refused credit at Madera.

1479

Columbus married, in Lisbon, Felipa Perestello Moniz, daughter of Bartolome Perestello and of his third wife, Isabel Moniz.

1480

Probable date of birth, in Porto Santo, of Diego Colon.

1482

In the period 1482-1485, in the service of Portugal, Columbus was at Mina. In a voyage from Lisbon to Guinea, he determined the latitude with the astrolabe and the quadrant as he would record later in his note, 490, in his copy of *Imago Mundi*: "I have observed the route carefully (as it is done by sailors and pilots) and after many trials of taking the height of the sun by using the quadrant and other instruments, I have found myself agreeing with Alfragan, that each degree corresponds to a distance equivalent to 56⅔ of a Roman mile."

1483
About this year, conversations are initiated between Columbus and Juan II of Portugal concerning the possibility of going to Asia by sailing to the West, starting from Lisbon.

1484
Felipa Perestello Moniz, wife of Columbus, died.

1485
The negotiations with Juan II of Portugal are ended. In the middle of this year, Columbus and his son, Diego, who was almost 5 years old, arrived at the monastery of La Rabida, coming from Lisbon where Columbus had been harassed by his creditors.

1486
At the beginning of May, the Queen Isabel received Columbus at the Alcazar of Cordova and listened with interest to his project, designating Fray Hernando de Talavera, her confessor, to organize a committee to decide about this project. At the end of the year, the first conversations between Columbus and this committee took place at Salamanca.

1487
The Treasury of Castilia gave to Columbus, on the 5th of May, 3,000 maravedises; the same quantity in July; 3,400 maravedises on August 27; and the same amount on October 15. The first donation was given in order that Columbus might go to the royal camp established near Malaga.

1488
March 20: Juan II of Portugal wrote to Columbus and called him his particular friend. In December, when Bartholomeu Dias came back from discovering the Cape of Good Hope, Columbus was in Lisbon as he mentions in his copy of *Imago Mundi*: "let the people know that in this year, 1488, in the month of December, Bartholomaeum Didacus arrived in Lisbon, captain of three caravels that his Royal Highness, the King of Portugal had sent to explore the land around the Cape of Good Hope, where he thought it was situated Agesinba (Abyssinia). He said that in this place, reached by use of the astrolabe, he was 45° below the equator (typical mistake of that era, the Cape is situated in 34° 21' S.). He described his trip and recorded it on a nautical chart, league by league, in order to be able to present this to the eyes of the King. I was present when this happened."
June 16: Columbus received 3,000 maravedises from the treasury of Castilia.
August 15: Fernando Columbus was born in Cordova.

1489
Columbus was among the besiegers of the town of Baza, that finally surrendered on the 4th of December. In order to go there, the kings had dictated, on

May 12, an order to all local functionaries to provide food and quarters for Columbus during his trip.

1490

Protected by Anne de Beaujeu, Bartolomeo Columbus presented his proposals to the court of France, but without success.

1491

Christopher Columbus ready to go to France, but he went first to La Rabida and here Fray Juan Perez promised him to intercede in his behalf to the Queen. The work of the monk was successful and the Queen sent Columbus 3,000 maravedises, so that Columbus could go to the court. At that time Martin Alonso Pinzon had already helped the future admiral.

1492

January 2: Granada surrendered and Columbus took part in the triumphant entry of the Catholic kings into the city. Afterwards, Columbus left the court when he saw that they had made no decision regarding his proposal, but Luis de Santangel being the secretary of rationing intervened decisively offering to finance the adventure. The Queen, highly impressed, promised that, if necessary, she would pawn her jewels in order to be able to carry out the projects of Columbus and ordered that a messenger go to look for him. This messenger finally found him in the small village of Pinos-Puente, near Santa Fe, where the royal camp was located.

April 17: The famous agreements in which are established the five articles of the reward that will be given to Columbus if he is successful in his adventure are signed in Santa Fe on this date. Other documents followed, dated April 30, the confirmation of his title and the credentials for the Grand Khan and other kings that he might find, as well as three orders for the armaments of the fleet, and a passport, this last without a date.

May 22: Columbus arrived in Palos in order to prepare for the expedition.

August 3: A little before sunrise, the little squadron started its trip. It was formed by the nao *Santa Maria,* with Columbus as captain and her owner Juan de la Cosa as master; the "round" caravel *Pinta,* captain Martin Alonso Pinzon, and Lateen Caravel *Nina,* captain Vicente Yanez Pinzon, brother of Martin Alonso.

August 12. Columbus arrived at the island of La Gomera with the *Santa Maria* and the *Nina* having previously ordered *Pinta* to enter the harbor of Las Palmas in order to repair her rudder.

August 25: Columbus arrived at Las Palmas where besides repairing the rudder of the *Pinta,* they changed the Lateen rig of the *Nina* to that of a "round" caravel.

September 1: Squadron sails from Las Palmas for La Gomera.

September 6: Squadron sails from La Gomera around to the westward.

September 16. The three vessels reached the Sea of Sargasso.

October 11: Signs of land evident at sunset.

October 12: Before daybreak, by the light of the moon, Rodrigo de Triana, lookout aboard the *Pinta,* which was (ranging) ahead, cried out Land! Land! and shortly therefater Martin Alonso ordered a shot to be fired with the lombard to notify the other vessels. On this day they landed at Bahia Long(a?), on the western coast of the island of San Salvador, called Guanahani by the Indians. The Admiral raised the Royal Standard and the captains the banners of the Green Cross. Roderigo de Escobedo, the Admiral's secretary, performed the act of taking possession of the island in the name of the King and Queen of Spain.

October 17: Columbus mentions in his Diary the Indians' hammocks, which were subsequently adopted by vessels throughout the world in place of the old bedplaces."

October 19: Squadron arrived at the island of Isabella, the Saometo of the Indians, today called Crooked Island.

October 21: Columbus identified Cipangu (Japan) with the island of Cuba, called Colba by the Indians, and according to the entry for this day determined to go "to Tierra firme (the mainland) and the city of Quisay — Quinsay — and to deliver the letters of their Highnesses to the Grand Khan, to obtain a reply and to return with it."

October 28: Arrived at the Bay of San Salvador, on the north coast of the island of Cuba, to which Columbus gave the name of Juana, in honor of the Infante (Prince) Don Juan, heir to the throne of Castile and Aragon.

November 6: Columbus noted in his Diary on the page corresponding to this day: "The two Christians found many people on the trail which went through its settlements, men and women with firebrands (tizon) in their hands, weeds (herbs, etc.) which they were accustomed to partake, for the aromatic smoke.

November 22: The *Pinta* separated from the rest of the fleet.

December 6: arrived at Port St. Nicholas on that Saint's day in the western extremity of what is today Haiti.

Sketch of north coast, Española, now Haiti, drawn by Christopher Columbus, 1492-3. Collection of the Duke of Alba.

December 13: Columbus made a mistake of about 14° in saying that by the quadrant, he had found that the latitude of the harbor of the Concepcion (Haiti) was 34° north (in reality it is 19° 35'). The mistake was made because he confused Polaris with another star, of the Cephus constellation.

December 25: At midnight the 24th the *Santa Maria*, ran aground on a coral reef in the Bay of Caracol (on the coast north of Hispaniola), and was destroyed. With the material they were able to save, the fort of La Navidad (the Nativity) was built, where 39 men remained under the command of Diego Arana, who was the master of arms of the fleet. The admiral transferred to the *Nina*, taking her as his flagship.

1493

January 6:   The *Pinta* comes into contact with the *Nina*.

January 16:   Columbus leaves the Gulf of the Arrows, on his return to Spain.

February 13:   On this date the *Nina* and the *Pinta* battle a heavy storm that separated them. The next day bad weather continued.

February 18:   The *Nina* anchored at the island of Santa Maria (the Azores).

February 19:   Joao de Castanheira, governor of the island of Santa Maria imprisons half of the crew of the *Nina* but later he sets them free.

February 24:   The *Nina* continued the return trip after this incident.

March 3:   A storm following the *Nina* reached its maximum intensity.

March 4:   Arrival of the *Nina* at Restello, the outer-harbor of Lisbon.

March 5:   Columbus arrived at Lisbon and conferred with Bartholomeu Dias and was later received by Juan II of Portugal.

March 13:   Columbus left Lisbon with the *Nina*.

March 15:   Around noon, the *Nina* arrived in Palos, completing the voyage of discovery. The *Pinta* had anchored in Bayona, near Vigo during the last days of February, and arrived in Palos the very same day as the *Nina*. The King, from Barcelona, congratulated Columbus for his success in the adventure and at the same time invited him to visit them and to prepare in Seville a new expedition.

April 15-20:   In this period Columbus arrived in Barcelona by an overland trip. He was received by the King and Queen in the room of the Tinell (Palace of the Kings of Aragon) and with a great demonstration of affection, they declared him a royal guest and made him a noble.

May 4:   Papal bull from Alejandro VI, following two others after May 3, by which was fixed the demarcation between the Spanish and Portuguese discoveries, by a line that passed 100 leagues west of the most western of the islands in the group of the Azores.

May 20:   The Catholic King presented Columbus with a coat of arms.

May 23:   Orders from the Catholic King stating that: "Every year 10,000 maravedises were to be given to Don Christopher Columbus for having been the first to discover the land in the Indies."

May 28:   Registered letter from the Catholic King naming Columbus Admiral of the Ocean Sea and Captain General of the squadron which was then being prepared for a new trip to the Indies.

September 25:   Columbus sailed from Cadiz on his second trip to the Indies with a squadron of 17 ships manned by 1,500 men. His flag ship had also the name *Santa Maria*, even though it was better known by the name of Marigalante." The caravel *Nina* was part of this squadron.

September 26:   New bull from Alejandro VI by which the rights of the Spaniards are enlarged to permit more discoveries to the west and south.

October 13.   The squadron of Columbus left the island of Hierro, sailing west, by one quarter to the southwest, (according to Cueno) looking for new lands.

November 3:   Columbus anchored in the island which he called Dominica, because it was reached on Sunday.   A little after sunrise he was able to see the island that later on he would baptize by the name "Santa Maria la Galante," "in honor of the ship in which he was sailing," according to Cuneo. The "Marigalante" seems to have been the most satisfactory of his four flag ships.

November 28:   After passing to the west of Sotavento islands and south of the group of the Eleven Thousand Virgins and San Juan Bautista (Puerto Rico), Columbus arrived at the fort of La Navidad and saw with sadness the destruction of the post he had left on his first trip.

1494

January 2:   Columbus established a base, later called "Isabella" in Cuba.

February 2:   Twelve ships commanded by Antonio Torres returned to Spain, arriving at Cadiz on March 7 with about 30,000 ducados of gold, 27 indians, and some cinnamon, pepper, wood and 60 parrots as "big as falcons."

April 24:   Columbus sailed from Cuba with three caravels: the *Nina* (flag ship), the *San Juan* and the *Cardera;* the last two of a capacity of about 40 toneles.   On board the *Nina* was Juan de la Cosa, the cartographer.   The purpose of Columbus, on this trip, was to "explore the main land of the Indians" and find the Grand Khan.

April 30:   The exploration of the south of Cuba began at the Bay of Guantanamo, where the U. S. Naval Base is located.   The bay was called Puerto Grande by Columbus.

May 5:   Arrival at Jamaica, which he explored until the 13th of the month and then went back to Cuba.

May 14:   The exploration of the coast of Cuba to Bahia Cortez began.

June 7:   Tordesillas Treaty between Spain and Portugal.   By which they accept, as a demarcation line between their respective discoveries a meridian at 370 leagues west of the Archipelago of Cape Verde.

June 13:   From Bahia Cortez Columbus began his return to "Isabella."

June 30:   The *Nina* ran aground in the Gulf of Batabano, but finally got off.

July 24 — September 29:   Return to Jamaica; Columbus explored the south side of this island and continued to the south of Espanola.   On passing El Paso de la Mona, the Admiral fell sick and his officers decided to return to "Isabella," where they disembarked Columbus, in a high fever and delirium. There they found Columbus' brother Bartolomeo, whom Columbus had not seen since he went to France.   Bartolomeo had arrived at "Isabella" with three Spanish caravels on the 24th of June.

End of 1494:   Four caravels loaded with supplies and commanded by Antonio Torres, arrived at "Isabella."

1495

February 24:   The four caravels of Antonio Torres sail from "Isabella" bound to Spain, carrying as passengers Michele Cuneo and Diego Colon.

April 3:   King Ferdinand ordered his overseer Juan Aguado to begin an investigation of the complaints received against Columbus and his brother.

June: A terrible hurricane destroyed most of the squadron of Columbus, except the *Nina* which was saved. In addition to the *San Juan, Cardera* and probably *La Gallega*, another caravel of 50 tons was built, launched under the name of *Santa Cruz,* better known as "La India" in honor of being the first ship constructed there.

August 5: The four caravels commanded by Juan Aguado sail from Seville and anchor at "Isabella" in October.

1496

March 10: Columbus leaves Isabella bound to Spain with the caravels *Nina* and *India*.

June 11: Columbus arrived at Cadiz returning from his second voyage.

July 12: The King and Queen send a letter to Columbus expressing their welcome on his return from the second voyage inviting him to visit them. During this time the Admiral lived in the house of Andres Bernaldez, to whom he confided the diaries of his second voyage and other documents that Bernaldez later used for his *History of the Catholic Kings.* Columbus was received by the royal family in Burgos and after informing them of his discoveries he proposed a third voyage be made.

1497

April 23: The Catholic King orders the third voyage of Columbus.

July 22: Bartolomeo Columbus was appointed Adelantado de las Indias and they gave him land concessions for purpose of cultivation on the island of Española (Dominica).

1498

February 18: The Queen appointed Fernando Colon as one of her pages. Diego Colon is also named as one of her pages.

February 22: Columbus willed the right of succession to his son Diego, and in case of death of Diego the order of succession will be: his son Fernando, his brother Bartolomeo and his oldest son, his brother Diego and his oldest son. The inheritance includes the title of Admiral and ⅛th of the gross profit from the products brought from the Indies.

May 30: Columbus sails from Sanlucar de Barrameda (Rio Gudalquivir) on his third voyage with six ships manned by 200 men. Three of the ships go directly to Santo Domingo, the new city on La Espanola. Columbus with the other three ships takes a direction more to the southward.

July 31: Columbus anchored at the island of Trinidad, which he named because of the three hills around the bay of Guayaguayare.

August 1: From the south side of Trinidad Columbus saw, for the first time, the American continent, the Punta Bombeador of Venezuela, which he took for an island and named it Sancta.

August 4: Columbus, after having noticed the effects of the currents of the river Orinoco, anchored behind the Cape of Lapa, also called Point of the Peninsula of Paria.

August 5. First landing in the American continent, probably at Yacua.

August 6: The ceremony taking possession at the river Guiria.

August 31: Arrival of Columbus at Santo Domingo after exploring the Gulf of Paria and passing west of the island Margarita. At Santo Domingo he was informed of the mutiny of Francisco Roldan.

October 18: Columbus sent two ships to Spain with news of his voyage and of the mutiny on the island.

1499

May 21: Royal decree signed in Madrid requiring that Commander Francisco de Bobadilla go to Española to impose royal authority and to punish rebels.

1500

August 23: Francisco de Bobadilla arrived at Santo Domingo.

October: Columbus and his brother Diego are sent to Spain in the caravel *Gorda* as prisoners. The captain of the caravel wished to unchain Columbus and his brother but they refused the favor.

November 25: Arrival at Cadiz of Columbus and his brother Diego.

December 12: Columbus and his two brothers are received by the King in the Alhambra de Granada; the royal family show them particular affection, especially the Queen, as it is said by Las Casas "because really she favored and defended him more than the King did and for that the Admiral had special confidence in her."

1501

September 3: Nicholas de Ovando was named Governor of the Indies.

September 17: Removed as the Governor of the Indies, Francisco de Bobadilla was called back to Spain.

1502

March 14: The Catholic King authorizes the fourth voyage of Columbus.

May 9: Columbus starts on his fourth voyage with four ships manned by 140 men. The admiral was accompanied by his son Fernando on board the flag-ship (official name not known). Bartolomeo Colon was on board the *Santiago de Palos*, nicknamed *La Bermuda*. The other two ships were *El Gallego* or *La Gallega* and *El Vizcaino* or *La Vizcaina*. Due to contrary and otherwise unfavorable winds, the little squadron, upon departure, took refuge in La Caleta until the 11th of May, when, with favorable winds, they finally departed.

May 25: Sailed from the Canaries, heading west.

June 15: Anchored at La Martinica, after a voyage of 21 days, which was the fastest of the four made by Columbus.

June 24: Columbus arrived at Santo Domingo, but the governor, Nicholas de Ovando did not permit him to disembark.

June 30: From the night of this day to July 1st, a severe hurricane occurred, as Columbus had predicted. The ships of his little squadron rode out the hurricane safely.

July 24: Columbus anchored off the island of San Juan Evangelista (Isle of Pines).

July 30: Arrival at the Bonacca, opposite Honduras.

August 14: From this date the ships beat to windward for 28 days in order to advance 170 miles to the Cape Gracias a Dios.

September 15: From this date to May 1, 1503, Columbus explored Nicaragua, Costa Rica, and Panama.

COLUMBUS' SHIPS

1503

January 20: By royal letters patent dated in Alcala de Henares, in Sevilla, Casa de Contratacion (House of Trade, Commerce and Traffic for the Indies) is founded.

June 25: Columbus arrived at Puerto Santa Gloria (Jamaica), but the two remaining caravels, the flag ship and the *Santiago,* are in such a deplorable state that he decided to run the ships aground. A man called Diego Mendez takes a heroic trip in a canoe from the ships to Española in search of aid.

1504

June 29: In a small caravel of the squadron of Mendez, under the command of Diego de Salcedo, Columbus and 100 men who survived the voyage sail from Jamaica, having remained on that island for a year and five days.

September 12: Columbus accompanied by his son and his brother left Santo Domingo, with Spain as their destination.

November 7: Columbus arrived at San Lucas de Barrameda.

November 26: Queen Isabella la Catolica died in Medina del Campo.

1505

February 23: By royal letters patent of the King Ferdnand, Columbus is authorized to travel by muleback and saddle. (The use of mules for transportation of persons was forbidden.)

1506

May 20: The discoverer of America died in Valladolid. Columbus was comforted in his last moments by his sons, all of whom were present: Diego, the heir to the titles, privileges and properties, and Fernando, his brother Diego. The brave Captain Diego Mendez, who in order to save Columbus in Jamaica took the risk of going to Santo Domingo in a fragile canoe, was also present.

Bibliography

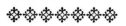

Anderson, R. C. — *The Rigging of Ships in the days of the Spritsail Topmast.* Salem, 1947.

" " " — *Seventeenth Century Rigging.* London, 1955.

" , Romola and R. C. — *The sailing ship. Six thousand years of history.* London, 1947.

Angherii, Petri Mertyris — *De Orbo Novo. Decade Tres.* 1516.

Arantegui y Sanz, Jose — *Apuntes historicos de la Artilleria espanola en los siglos XIV, XV y XVI.* Madrid, 1887-91.

Artinano G. de — *La Arquitectura Naval Espanola.* Madrid, 1920.

Ashley, Clifford W. — *The Ashley book of knots.* London, 1947.

Ballesteros, Antonio — *Historia de America.* Volume V. *Cristobal Colon y el descubrimiento de America.*

Bowen, Frank C. — *From Carrack to Clipper.* London, 1927.

Brito, N. de — *Caravelas, Naus d Gales de Portugal.* Oporto.

Cano, Thome — *Arte para fabricar, fortificar y aparejar naos de guerra y merchantes; con las reglas para Archearlas, redusidas a la Cuenta y Medida; y en grande utulidad de la navegacion.* Seville, 1611.

Concas, V. — *Desde la nao "Santa Maria."* Madrid, 1893.

Correia, Jose Candido — *Memoria acerca das Construcoes e Armamentos* Lisbon, 1888.

Crescentio — Nautica Mediterranea. Rome 1602.

Chaves, Alonso de — *Cosmographia pratica.* Manuscript with no date, located in the library of the Royal Academy of History, Madrid. (Written between 1520 and 1538.)

D'Albertis, E. — *Le costruzioni navale e l'arte de la navigazione al tempo de*

C. Colombo. Volume IV de la *Raccolta di Documenti e Studi pubblicati dalla R. Commissione Colombiana.* Rome, 1892-1894.

Du Cange — *Glossarium ad scriptores mediae et infimae latinitatis. Paris,* 1773.

Escalante de Mendoza, Johan — *Itinerario de Nevagacion de los mares y tierras Occidentales.* Manuscipt 1585.

Etayo, Carlos — *La "Santa Maria," la "Nina" y la "Pinta."* Pamplona, 1962.

Fernandez Duro, Cesaro — *Disquisiciones nauticas.* Volume I. Madrid, 1877.

"   "   "   *Carabelas. Estudios hechos sobre los disenos que se conservan en varias obras antiguas.* Madrid, 1892.

"   "   "   *Primer viaje de Colon.* Madrid, 1892.

"   "   "   and Monleon, Rafael — *La nao "Santa Maria," capitana de Colon.*

"   "   "   Memory of the Executive Archeological Commission. Madrid, 1892.

Fernandez de Navarrete, Martin — *Coleccion de Viajes.* Madrid, 1825.

Fernandes, Manuel — *Livro das tracas de Carpinteria.* 1616. Library of Ajuda. Manuscript, 60 text pages, large format and 74 pages of drawings. Dr. Sousa Viterbo discovered it and in his work *Trabalhos Nauticos dos Portugueses nos seculos XVI y XVII* says that Fernandes is "the most celebrated technician in naval construction." This important graphical document is the only one on the architecture of the caravel even though we may be sorry that its author did not make the drawing of the rigging as well.

Fonseca, Quirino da — *A caravela portuguesa. E a pioridade tecnica das navegacoes henriquinas.* Coimbra, 1934.

Fontoura da Costa — *A marinharia dos descobrimentos.* Lisbon, 1934.

Furttenbach, J. — *Architectura Navalis.* Ulm, 1629. Facsimile, Paris, 1939.

Galiano, Dionisio Alcala — "La carabela 'Gallega' o 'Santa Maria,' o la nao capitana de Colon." *Revista General de Marina,* October, 1892.

"   "   "   *Nueva consideraciones sobre les carabelas de Colon.* Madrid, 1893.

Garcia del Palacio — *Instruccion Nautica.* Mexico, 1587. First nautical treatise published in America.

Guillen Tato, Julio F. — *La carabela "Santa Maria."* Madrid, 1927.

"   "   "   "   "Naos y carabelas." *Revista General de Marina,* Madrid, 1942.

"   "   "   "   *El primer viaje de Cristobal Colon.* Madrid, 1943.

"   "   "   "   *Por que Cristobal Colon vino a la Rabida.* Madrid, 1944.

"   "   "   "   *La parla marinera en el Diario del primer viaje de Cristobal Colon.* Madrid, 1951.

Jal, Auguste — *Archeologie Navale.* Paris, 1840.

"   "   *Glossaire Nautique.* Paris, 1848.

Laird, Clowes, G. S. — *Sailing Ships. Their history and development as illustrated by the collection of ship-models in the Science Museum. Part I. Historical notes.* Science Museum. London, 1932.

"   "   "   "   *Sailing Ships.* Part II. *Catalogue of Exhibits with descriptive notes.* Science Museum. London, 1952.

Landstrom, Bjorn. — *The Ship.* 1961.

Las Casas, Bartolome de — *Historia de las Indias.* Madrid, 1875.

Laughton, L. G. Carr — *Old Ships, Figure-Heads and Sterns.* London, 1925.

Livro Nautico — Collection of manuscripts existent in the National Library of Lisbon. In great part in relation to nautical matters of the end of the 16th century. In some of them we find the dates of 1575, 1580 to 1589, and 1591.

Martinez-Hidalgo, Jose Ma. — *Historia y leyenda de la aguja magnetica. Contribucion de los espanoles al progreso de la nautica.* Barcelona, 1946.

"   "   "   "   *Del remo a la vela.* Barcelona, 1948.

"   "   "   "   "Naos y carabelas." Article in *La Vanguardia.* Barcelona, June 3, 1951.

"   "   "   "   *Enciclopedia General del Mar.* Barcelona, 1957.

"   "   "   "   *A bordo de la "Santa Maria." Hombres y naves del Descubrimiento.* Barcelona, 1961.

Mendonca, Henrique Lopes de — *Estudo sobre of Navios Portuguese nos seculos XV, XVI.* Lisbon, 1892.

Monleon, Rafael — "Las carabelas de Colon." In *El Centenario,* Volume I. Madrid, 1892.

"   "   "La carabela 'Santa Maria'". *In Revista General de Marina,* Volume XXVIII.

"   "   *Restauracion hipotetica de las carabelas de Colon.* Madrid, 1891.

Moore, Alan — "Rig in northern Europe." Separate of *The Mariner's Mirror,* February, 1956.

Morison, Samuel Eliot — *El Almirante de la Mar Oceano.* Buenos Aires, 1945.

Morton, Nancy R. — "The Ship of the Renaissance." Separate of *The Mariner's Mirror,* August and November 1955.

"   "   "   *Sailing-Ships Models.* London, 1949.

Nouhuys, I. W. van — *Het model van een Spanisch Karveel uit het begin der 15.* Museum Prins Hendrik. Rotterdam, 1929.

Oliveira, Joao Braz de — "Navios Portugueses do tempo dos Descobrimentos e Conquistas." *In Revista Portuguesa Colonial e Maritima,* No. 8, May, 1898.

Vivielle, G. y La Roerie, J. — *Navires at Marins. De la rame a l'Helice.* Brussels, 1930.

COLUMBUS' SHIPS

Winter, Heinrich — *Breydenbachs Pilgerreise nach dem heiligen Lande, 1486.* Berlin, 1930.

„   „   *Die Katalanische Nao von 1450.* Magdeburg, 1956.

„   „   *Das Hanseschiff im ausgehenden 15. Jahrhundert.* Leipzig, 1961.

General Index

COLUMBUS' SHIPS